Advertising in a Free Society

Advertising in a Free Society

RALPH HARRIS

ARTHUR SELDON

with an introduction by

CHRISTOPHER SNOWDON

The Institute of Economic Affairs

First published in Great Britain in 1959
and this edition published in Great Britain in 2014 by
The Institute of Economic Affairs
2 Lord North Street
Westminster
London SW1P 3LB
in association with London Publishing Partnership Ltd
www.londonpublishingpartnership.co.uk

The mission of the Institute of Economic Affairs is to improve understanding of the fundamental institutions of a free society by analysing and expounding the role of markets in solving economic and social problems.

A CIP catalogue record for this book is available from the British Library.

ISBN 978-0-255-36696-0

Many IEA publications are translated into languages other than English or are reprinted. Permission to translate or to reprint should be sought from the Director General at the address above.

Typeset in Kepler by T&T Productions Ltd
www.tandtproductions.com

Originally printed in Great Britain by The Stellar Press Ltd

CONTENTS

THE AUTHOR

Christopher Snowdon is director of lifestyle economics at the Institute of Economic Affairs. His research focuses on lifestyle freedoms, prohibition and policy-based evidence. He is an occasional contributor to City AM and Spiked, and regularly appears on TV and radio discussing social and economic issues.

Snowdon's work encompasses a diverse range of topics including 'sin taxes', state funding of charities, happiness economics, 'public health' regulation, gambling and the black market. He is also the author of *The Art of Suppression: Pleasure, Panic and Prohibition since 1800* (2011), *The Spirit Level Delusion* (2010) and *Velvet Glove, Iron Fist: A History of Anti-Smoking* (2009).

FOREWORD

It is a pleasure to see the Institute of Economic Affairs republish an abridged version of a pioneering work that may have been the first principled explanation of the role of advertising in a free society.

In the late 1950s, Ralph Harris and Arthur Seldon – the founders of the IEA – were concerned about the attacks on advertising, especially influential critiques by American writers Vance Packard and John Kenneth Galbraith. As students of free markets, Harris and Seldon knew that advertising was simply an element of a functioning market system. It didn't need condemnation – or glorification. Rather, it had a valuable role in serving consumers as well as producers; if it hadn't, it would have disappeared.

Yet the reigning economists of the day, in both the United States and Great Britain, eschewed objective analysis of advertising. Instead, they treated it as a deceptive add-on to more acceptable economic functions such as production and distribution.

So, with little support from the academy, these two young men took up the challenge of explaining the role of advertising. And, unlike academic economists, they did so in a very public way. There was no hiding behind academic tomes or journals! Publication of this book required some courage.

While the message of the book stands just as tall today as it did then, Christopher Snowdon, the editor of the current volume, has made the book particularly relevant. He has written a magisterial introduction and has seamlessly edited out discussions of Harris and Seldon's original text that would sound too dated or narrow. He retains, however, some of the historical character of the work, such as the rather charming appendix on the subject of detergent advertising. Amusing though such controversy may seem now, the apparent triviality and repetitiveness of detergent advertising had become something of a cause célèbre and a focus for anti-advertising harangues.

I had the opportunity to meet both Ralph Harris and Arthur Seldon in the 1980s and had the privilege of getting to know Arthur and his wife, Marjorie (who, I discovered, had written a beautiful memoir, *Poppies and Roses*). My husband, Richard Stroup, is an economist and was a co-founder of the Property and Environment Research Center (PERC) in Bozeman, Montana. PERC was one of a growing number of institutes applying classical liberal scholarship to issues of the day – to such fields as the environment, education, tax policy, etc.

Arthur respected Richard as one of the younger economists who were no longer in thrall to Keynesianism. We, of course, recognised Arthur's critical role in bringing back free-market ideas to Great Britain through the Institute of Economic Affairs. At that time, the IEA's impact on Prime Minister Margaret Thatcher's thinking about policy had become well known, and the IEA was viewed as a model for the increasing number of 'think tanks' in the United States.

The defence of free markets is a job that is never finished. That is why this book, in its new form, will be a valuable reference for responding to present and future attacks against advertising. By laying out the arguments against advertising and steadfastly responding with temperate analysis, Ralph Harris and Arthur Seldon, aided now by Christopher Snowdon, set a high standard for explaining the benefits of free enterprise.

This book will be another reminder of why markets are the best way for a society to organise and why we are all fortunate when they are allowed to operate with a minimum of coercive control. I'm honoured to have the opportunity to welcome *Advertising in a Free Society.*

JANE S. SHAW
President
John W. Pope Center for Higher Education Policy
Raleigh, North Carolina, USA

July 2014

The views expressed in this monograph are, as in all IEA publications, those of the author and not those of the Institute (which has no corporate view), its managing trustees, Academic Advisory Council members or senior staff. With some exceptions, such as with the publication of lectures, all IEA monographs are blind peer-reviewed by at least two academics or researchers who are experts in the field.

SUMMARY

- In practice it is impossible to distinguish between advertising that is intended to be persuasive and advertising that is intended to be informative. Persuasive advertising normally has information content and even basic information provided by a company about its products will normally be intended to make consumers more interested in the product.
- Advertising is more likely to reduce, rather than increase, costs and prices. Advertising increases the extent of the markets in which companies are able to operate, therefore leading to greater economies of scale. This is confirmed by the empirical evidence.
- Advertising effectively subsidises the press and broadcast media.
- It is a mistake to regard advertising as a waste of resources which, if it were regulated, could be eliminated. Businesses have to transmit information about products in one way or another. If they did not advertise, they would have to find other – probably more expensive – ways to do this.
- There is no evidence that advertising creates monopolies. Indeed, if anything, advertising increases competition by improving information to consumers.

- Advertising is less of a reflection of corporate power than of corporate vulnerability. Advertising tends to be used by established companies as a way of building brand loyalty.
- The evidence suggests that advertising is not manipulative in any meaningful sense. It is not an important determinant of consumer behaviour, though it can help build brand loyalty. Certainly, advertising does not effectively contrive 'wants' in the way suggested by critics such as J. K. Galbraith.
- All serious studies of the advertising of alcohol and tobacco suggest that it has the same impact on the overall consumption of these products as on the consumption of any other product: none. This is a conclusion that is at odds with the assertions of political campaigners.
- An attack on advertising is, in effect, an attack on free speech. While commercial free speech may not be valued as highly by some as other forms of free speech, it should, nevertheless, be defended as an important principle.
- Ironically, though it is politicians who are responsible for any prohibition or limitation of advertising, it is advertising by politicians themselves that Harris and Seldon found to be systematically and incorrigibly dishonest.

PART 1

INTRODUCTION TO
ADVERTISING IN A FREE SOCIETY

CHRISTOPHER SNOWDON

1 BACKGROUND

Written by Ralph Harris and Arthur Seldon, *Advertising in a Free Society* was first published in 1959, two years after Vance Packard's best-selling exposé of motivational research in advertising, *The Hidden Persuaders,* and one year after J. K. Galbraith portrayed advertising as the driver of needless consumption in *The Affluent Society.* In Britain, rationing had finally come to an end five years earlier and it was two years since Harold Macmillan had announced that 'most of our people have never had it so good'. The first television commercial (for 'tingling fresh' toothpaste) had been broadcast just four years earlier, on 2 September 1955. In the US, the advertising industry was firmly in its *Mad Men* era, the first series of which is set in 1960, but even the marketing executives of Madison Avenue and Soho, so skilled at putting their clients' products in the best light, seemed unable to lift the reputation of their own industry.

Advertising was widely seen as trivial, repetitive and dishonest. It was disparaged by conservatives for being economically wasteful and despised by many socialists for being the garish face of capitalism. It was rarely defended, except – grudgingly – as a necessary evil that helped subsidise the media. Today, as in 1959, advertising continues to attract what Harris and Seldon described as 'many weighty criticisms'. For those who view it as capitalist propaganda, advertising bears the brunt of attacks that might more openly be made against the free market. For those who object to consumerism, marketing is held responsible for manipulating the public into buying products they neither want nor need. For those who reject the concept of consumer sovereignty, advertisers 'use every possible trick and tactic to catch us hapless flies in their profit-driven webs' (Hastings 2013: 151).

In *Advertising in a Free Society*, Harris and Seldon undertook a thorough review of what was then a subject largely ignored by economists. Empirical research into the economic effects of advertising was in its infancy and the authors lamented in the preface that there were 'not many economist writers on advertising whom we found directly helpful'. Since advertising was considered a rather grubby part of the economic landscape, what little academic attention it received tended to come from critics. Harris and Seldon divided advertising's opponents into the 'classical critics', such as the renowned economist Alfred Marshall, and the 'left-wing critics', notably Nicholas Kaldor, whose 1950 study *The Economics of Advertising* continues to be widely cited in the academic literature today. They also addressed the social critics, notably John Kenneth Galbraith, whose then recently published book *The Affluent Society* had been an instant commercial success.

Looking back, it is remarkable how little the arguments against advertising have changed. Empirical research has taken the wind out of many of the economic objections, but aside from a greater focus on the alleged environmental impact of mass consumption, the social criticisms remain much the same (and, as Harris and Seldon point out, they were far from new even in the 1950s).

In addition to reviewing the economic literature, Harris and Seldon carried out detailed research into the marketing plans of many British industries from banking and brewing to hair perms and pet food. Despite a number of criticisms and caveats, they concluded that advertising was not a necessary evil but a necessary good that was beneficial to both the consumer and the producer. It greased the wheels of capitalism, opened the eyes of consumers and led to greater efficiency in markets. Contrary to the classical and left-wing critics, Harris and Seldon argued that advertising 'has helped to keep markets competitive, tumbled oligopolists and monopolists, kept prices down, and in the long run made the economic system bow to the consumer's will'. If, as some critics complained, advertising created new desires, that was to be celebrated, not condemned.

In this introduction, we shall examine how well Harris and Seldon's arguments stand up half a century later.

2   THE ECONOMIC EVIDENCE

Economic evidence: the consumer

In the decades since *Advertising in a Free Society* was first published, a large amount of empirical evidence has been produced that generally, albeit sometimes tentatively, supports Harris and Seldon's view of advertising as being economically beneficial. The key economic questions raised by the classical and left-wing critics were whether advertising raised prices, created barriers to entry or was an inefficient use of a firm's money. Left-wing critics were particularly concerned that advertising allowed companies to benefit from the mass market without passing on the savings to the consumer. Classical critics, on the other hand, were concerned that branding and marketing made demand less elastic and therefore made competition more imperfect. Both sets of critics feared that 'combative' advertising, in which companies battle for a share of a static market, was economically wasteful and therefore likely to lead to higher prices.

Academic discussions of advertising have traditionally made a distinction between the 'informative' and the 'persuasive'. Informative advertising of the sort that might be seen in a newspaper's small ads was generally considered useful while persuasive advertising, which dwelt on minor differences between brands and sought to sell a product by selling a lifestyle, was considered inefficient and unnecessary. Few denied that consumers benefited from being made aware of a product's existence, but since the essential information in an advert extends little further than the price, specification and location of the vendor, there was a residual prejudice against the supposedly 'wasteful' advertising which hammered home the same old brands.

This argument is still made today, but it received short shrift from Harris and Seldon, who argued that it is impossible to draw a distinction between 'informative advertising' and 'persuasive advertising' in practice. No matter how much information an advertisement contains, its purpose is to persuade (Harris and Seldon noted that 'even a railway timetable is meant to encourage travelling by train'). Conversely, a 'persuasive' advertisement contains information, even if it is only the name of the brand or the price of the product. The simplest advertisements for well-known brands remind consumers of the product's existence and make them recall information that they have received in previous advertisements, reviews, personal recommendations or past experience.

Schmalensee (2008) summarises the critics' position as follows: 'Buyers are assumed to respond rationally to informative advertisements, while persuasive advertisements are somehow manipulative.' However, he concludes that 'this distinction is of little value empirically: few if any advertisements present facts in a neutral fashion with no attempt to persuade, and even those with no obvious factual content signal to consumers that the seller has invested money to get their attention.' There is no denying that many advertisements lean more heavily on gimmicks, jingles and humour than on hard facts, but this is necessary if the message is to be remembered. Information is no use if it goes unnoticed or is forgotten (Kirzner 1971).

With regards to pricing, there is very little evidence to suggest that advertising raises the cost of products and much to suggest that lower prices are typical. None of the studies which examine places that forbid advertising for certain products find lower prices than in places where advertising is allowed (Benham 1972; Cady 1976; Kwoka 1984; Milyo and Waldfogel 1999; Clark 2007). On the contrary, prices in jurisdictions where advertising is allowed tend to be lower. Moreover, it is usually the case that 'prices of advertised products are lower than those not advertised' (Schmalensee 2008). Love and Stephen's review of the literature on the self-regulating professions found that advertising is associated with lower fees (Love and Stephen 1996) and, in a thorough review of the literature, Kyle Bagwell (2007: 51) found 'substantial evidence that retail advertising leads to lower prices' in many industries as well as 'some evidence' that manufacturer advertising also leads to lower prices.

Economic evidence: the producer

The question of whether advertising is efficient is partly answered by its tendency to make prices lower. The cost of advertising can be recouped with an appropriate return from the greater sales that come from economies of scale and selling over a wider area to a larger customer base. Businesses must believe that advertising is a more efficient way of selling than, for example, employing travelling salesmen or else they would not advertise. They would be victims of an enormous global information failure if they were wrong in this belief. If companies prefer to use advertising, rather than telesales teams or discount coupons, it is a good indication that advertising is more effective and efficient.

But advertising does not necessarily have to lead to more sales for it to be efficient. It merely needs to be cheaper than the alternative. Critics who count advertising spend, which typically represents 1–2 per cent of GDP, as wasteful expenditure appear to forget that companies would need to find other ways to sell in the absence of advertising. Their criticisms of advertisers resemble the old complaints about 'middlemen', such as investors and wholesalers, who have historically been portrayed as parasites who take profit without adding value. But as Harris and Seldon note, the retailer, wholesaler, salesman and advertiser are as integral to commerce as the craftsman and the labourer. Selling is a legitimate cost of doing business and it would be wrong to exclude advertising from a firm's expenses when calculating taxable profits or to tax it, as some socialist writers have suggested (Korten 2001: 269; Murphy 2011: 287).

Advertising would not survive for long if it consistently led to lower profits and so it is no surprise to find that economic studies have shown a strong tendency towards greater profitability, particularly in the case of products that are purchased frequently ('convenience goods') (Comanor and Wilson 1967, 1974; Weiss 1969). However, this is not always the case and some studies have observed the opposite effect (Bloch 1974; Ayanian 1975). The much-quoted analysis, usually attributed to Lord Leverhulme, that 'half of every advertising appropriation is wasted, but nobody knows which half' may explain why the empirical evidence is mixed. Some advertising campaigns are duds and some products are in irreversible decline regardless of the quality of their advertising.

It seems likely, therefore, that there are some markets in which advertising reduces company profits, especially if companies are locked in a prisoner's dilemma in which they feel forced to advertise because their competitors are advertising (Frank 1999: 155–56; Qi 2013). For Harris and Seldon, this was just too bad. Capitalism exists to serve the buyer, not the seller. If advertising increases profits then so much the better, but the real question is whether it lowers prices and spreads information. Generally speaking, it does. Furthermore, it benefits consumers by saving time and reducing search costs. As Harris and Seldon point out, there are times when 'the consumer may not wish to be bothered with the business of acquiring more information'. Consumers might be prepared to spend time researching a product when it involves major expenditure, but they are 'prepared to leave the choice of their bootlaces or bathpowder to agents: retailers whose advice and judgement they have learned to respect, or manufacturers whose brands they have learned to trust'.

And why not? Bagwell (2007: 41) argues that consumers are less responsive to advertising when products are of higher price and bought less frequently because they are prepared to 'incur meaningful search costs in order to obtain better information'. But when it comes to convenience goods, consumers have little to lose by trying a product on the basis of an advertisement. Trusted brands are, say Harris and Seldon, 'the consumers' guarantee'. The existence of costly advertising gives the customer an assurance – rarely unjustified – that the product's manufacturers 'are not will-o-the-wisps, barrow-boys who are here today and gone tomorrow.' The time-saving benefits advertising provide to the consumer by helping him separate the wheat from the chaff are an important, though largely overlooked, aspect of advertising.

3 DOES ADVERTISING CREATE MONOPOLIES?

Advertising and market power

The combination of lower prices and higher profits appears to create an incongruous win–win situation. Is advertising such a panacea that it enables consumers to buy at lower prices while helping companies to make larger profits? To answer this, we must ask what happens when advertising works (which, it must be restated, is not always).

Advertising creates economies of scale by extending a company's reach across the country and beyond. It facilitates direct selling to the consumer by mail order or over the Internet, thereby cutting costs. It helps the most efficient companies to thrive at the expense of the more wasteful. It allows innovative products to appear on the shelves in lightning quick time. In short, it makes a low-cost mass market possible. These efficiencies enable companies to lower prices, but it cannot be denied that the arrival of large corporations selling global brands often comes at the expense of some small, local companies which do not or cannot compete at the same level. It is therefore plausible that advertising wipes out competition and could ultimately lead to monopoly.

The fear of incumbent firms using advertising to keep out competitors was a concern for classical critics such as Alfred Marshall and Arthur Pigou. On the other hand, advertising might afford new entrants the tools they need to break into the market. The empirical evidence has produced mixed results with regards to whether advertising facilitates or deters new entrants in the market, but it seems to make markets more competitive most of the time (Bagwell 2007: 45–47).

Incumbent businesses sometimes increase their advertising spend in response to the arrival of a newcomer (Thomas 1999; Alemson 1970) and Harris and Seldon believed that advertising could indeed be used by 'dominant retailers' to keep out competitors. However, even if this were the case, they did not believe that *all* competitors could be kept out. Advertising *might* lead to an oligopoly of large firms dominating the market, but critics were wrong to assume that 'oligopoly is one degree removed from monopoly.' So long as the oligopoly remains competitive and does not turn into a cartel, the consumer would not suffer. Each company would continue to compete fiercely on price and quality to the consumer's benefit. There are a limited number of supermarket chains in the UK, for instance, but few would argue that there is no competition, let alone that the supermarket oligopoly is a virtual monopoly that keeps prices high. Harris and Seldon made the comparison with democracy, noting that the [then] 'British "two-party" system is not merely one degree removed from totalitarianism; it is democracy in action.'

The tendency towards lower prices mentioned above strongly suggests that market concentration driven by advertising creates neither cartels nor monopolies. This can be illustrated by a fact Harris and Seldon mention, almost in passing, in Appendix A. They note that the four largest makers of detergent accounted for 28 per cent of sales in 1948, but this had risen to 97 per cent just eight years later. This dramatic change in market concentration is not unusual for a new product category (as washing powder was in the 1940s). It can be compared with the market concentration of Internet search engines at the turn of the millennium or the appearance of an oligopoly in cigarette companies in the early twentieth century. It is common for the number of producers to be whittled down in the early days of a new market as the least efficient firms exit or are taken over. Advertising can play a role in this, but – and this is Harris and Seldon's main point – *it does not lead to monopoly.* The market for washing detergents remains fiercely competitive in Britain half a century later and the same cigarette companies continue to fight for market share globally. Even Google, with its two-thirds share of the world's search engine traffic, cannot afford to be complacent. No matter how many users a free-to-consumer website has, it never has a monopoly, let alone an unshakeable monopoly, so long as rival services exist, or can come into being. The 2007 *Guardian* article 'Will Myspace ever lose its monopoly?'[1] stands as a warning to those who mistake temporary market share for enduring

---

1   Older readers may recall Myspace as a forerunner to Facebook.

power (Keegan 2007). So long as the market is contestable, there is competitive pressure to keep prices down, even if there are only one or two 'dominant retailers' (Armentano 1999).

According to one of advertising's most virulent contemporary critics, marketing is 'how the corporation gets its power' (Hastings 2013), but what kind of 'power' is it? Although it is often claimed that a dominant retailer 'controls' a certain percentage of the market, this is an illusion (imagine a politician saying that his party controls 35 per cent of the electorate!). On this, it is worth revisiting Naomi Klein's 2000 book, *No Logo*, a fiery polemic against the supposedly growing power of 'superbrands', to see how many 'powerful' and 'omnipresent' multinationals have since fallen on hard times. Blockbuster, which Klein said 'controls 25 per cent of the home-video market' found that its dominance was no protection when it filed for bankruptcy in 2010 (see also Kodak, which 'controlled' 80 per cent of the US photographic film market in the 1990s before filing for bankruptcy in 2012). Among the other firms name-checked in *No Logo* are Borders (declared bankrupt in 2011), General Motors (filed for bankruptcy in 2009), Benetton (withdrew from 25 countries in 2013), Tommy Hilfiger (lost more than half its market value between 1999 and 2006 before being sold) and Netscape (disbanded in 2003). The Gap clothing chain, which seemed unstoppable when Klein wrote her book, was described as a 'struggling retailer' by the *New York Times* when it announced plans to close a fifth of its US stores in 2011. Fifteen years on, Microsoft no longer has what Klein called a 'near monopoly' and few would echo her claim that Apple's products are 'mere filler for the real production: the brand' (Klein 2000: 15–16).

The might of the Ford Motor Company was not enough to sell the notorious Edsel car, the 'power' of Coca-Cola could not sell New Coke, and Google's market dominance could not make Google Plus a success. The list of dominant retailers failing to sell heavily advertised new products is endless, as is the list of seemingly invincible companies going to the wall. As Harris and Seldon write in *Advertising in a Free Society*, it is the consumer who retains 'the ultimate power of veto'. The consumer remains sovereign.

Widening the extent of the market

An important subtlety is often missed in the debate about large firms and market power. It may be true that advertising allows larger firms to compete more effectively with smaller local firms – while also facilitating the entry of later challengers to those larger firms. This can lead to economies of scale and lower prices but need not increase market power. The effect of this process is not to replace a situation where (for example) six small local firms were competing with each other with a situation where there is one large firm benefiting from economies of scale. Instead, the larger firms operate over a much wider area as a result of being able to advertise and challenge incumbents. There can be many such large firms operating in these wider markets. Supermarkets are the obvious example here. Six or more supermarkets compete vigorously across national – and sometimes international – markets, whereas, in previous eras, a small number of small firms competed in small local markets. Indeed, it is worth noting that, in the era of the small shop, direct competition between shops of the same type was rare and, insofar as competition between large supermarkets is inhibited today, it is as a result of planning controls.

4 BRAND LOYALTY, ADDED VALUE AND MANIPULATION

Added value and brand loyalty

Among the classical critics' concerns about advertising was the fear that brand loyalty created 'reputational monopolies' which made demand less elastic and took the market further from the ideal of perfect competition. This, in turn, could lead to monopoly. But, while advertising by a single company seeks to create brand loyalty, advertising as a whole seeks to create disloyalty. The essence of 'combative' advertising is to encourage brand switching: it encourages consumers to sample a company's offering and, if they like it, stick with it until they are tempted by some other brand. Evidence shows that we are becoming more, not less, tempted to switch brands in the age of 'superbrands'. *The Economist* noted in 2001 that brand loyalty had declined amongst every generation since the 1970s: 'The result is that many of the world's biggest brands are struggling. If they are making more and more noise, it is out of desperation' (*The Economist* 2001).

The ubiquity of advertising in the modern world is not a reflection of corporate power, as some have argued, but of vulnerability. Much advertising is defensive, which is to say that it seeks to keep existing customers buying the product, but this is only necessary because other companies are doing everything they can to encourage disloyalty. 'Contrary also to what the critics assert,' writes Kirkpatrick (1994: 168), 'advertising creates disloyalty in consumers, not brand loyalty. The product creates the loyalty.' Moreover, the price premium charged for heavily advertised brands creates opportunities for competitors to beat the big producers on price (retailers' own brands do this with conspicuous success). So while advertising might raise barriers to entry in one area, it can lower barriers to entry in another.

These are basically the arguments made by the Chicago economists in the 1960s, a few years after Harris and Seldon took a similar position in *Advertising in a Free Society*. They argued that advertising is pro-competitive because it spreads information and gives new entrants a way to announce themselves. On the question of whether advertising raises or lowers barriers to entry, the empirical evidence is mixed (perhaps because pro-competitive and anti-competitive effects can be seen in different circumstances), but it generally supports the view that advertising 'is frequently a means of entry and a sign of competition' (Telser 1964: 558).

The marketing of big, familiar brands, often with minimal slogans ('Just do it', 'I'm lovin' it', etc.) is pure combative advertising aimed at reinforcing the brand's 'personality' so that we remember it. Personalising brands can be done by emphasising unique characteristics, or by focusing on a particular characteristic that its rivals underplay, or by creating a memorable identity such as Tony the Tiger, the Jolly Green Giant and the Michelin man. The complaint of critics over the decades has been that, if we were not tricked by the marketing men into believing that there was a major difference between largely homogeneous goods, we would enjoy products of similar quality without paying a premium price. The argument against global brands therefore encompasses traditional concerns about the wastefulness of combative advertising alongside more modern concerns about 'hyper-consumerism'.

Harris and Seldon respond to this in two ways. Firstly, they say that products are not homogeneous. An unbranded shirt may be of similar quality to a Fred Perry shirt, but this is by no means guaranteed. Branding, they say, 'is essentially a grading device which helps the public to identify a particular product and to associate it with an expected quality, taste or other standard of performance.' The greater the value of the brand, the greater is the incentive for the manufacturer to keep standards high. A company that has invested millions of pounds building a brand is playing for higher stakes than a fly-by-night market trader. It cannot afford the bad publicity that will come from selling shoddy goods.[1] As the classical economist Alfred Marshall noted in 1919, a company's investment in a brand means that 'measures are taken to prevent the goods from being sold in poor condition, and thus bringing the brand into disfavour among consumers' (Marshall 1919: 302).

---

1   As the experience of many car companies has shown over the decades when they have brought out models that have been defective in some way.

But what if it could be shown that the more expensive branded good is identical to the unbranded budget good by objective criteria? Would this not be proof that the company is playing on consumers' vanity and anxiety to exploit them? Harris and Seldon argue that the question is meaningless because a product has no objective value. Even if the branded good is distinguishable from the unbranded good only by the advertising that portrays it as being of higher class, the consumer is justified in buying it. If he values it more highly because he associates it with glamour, good taste or ethical living then he is right to pay more for it. Harris and Seldon argue that 'if a bath soap, a fountain-pen, or a carpet gives more pleasure when the consumer thinks it is used by a duchess or a television performer, then he is making a logical decision in buying it: he is being more sensible than his critics'.

If advertising can turn a humdrum item into a mark of class and distinction, the advertiser has added value, as Jamie Whyte (2007) explains:

> If I messed with your head so that you found standing on one leg immensely enjoyable, then I would have improved standing on one leg [...] There are two ways to improve a product: change its material properties or change the way consumers respond to it. Advertising works in the second way. In many cases it is fantastically successful. The pleasure of consuming some products, such as Chanel perfume and Nike trainers, is largely due to their brands. Why bemoan this fact? Why regret that advertising works? When it does, it makes things better.

In any case, there is little evidence that the public are being systematically duped into buying inferior products at extortionate prices. The modern shopper has a range of magazines (for example, *Which?*) and television shows (for example, *Watchdog*) as well as money-saving experts and consumer protection organisations to turn to for advice. The public are not fools: 'It is often charged that advertising can persuade people to buy inferior products', wrote the British advertising magnate David Ogilvy. He continued: 'So it can – once. But the consumer perceives that the product is inferior and never buys it again. This causes financial loss to the manufacturer, whose profits come from repeat purchases' (Ogilvy 2007: 215). This common sense view was held by Alfred Marshall when he wrote that advertising is 'seldom of much value, unless accompanied by capable and honourable dealing [...] no amount of expenditure in advertising will enable any thing, which the customers can fairly test for themselves by experience (this condition excludes medicines which claim to be appropriate to subtle diseases, etc.[2]), to get a permanent hold on the people, unless it is fairly good relative to its price' (Marshall 1919: 306).

The classic example of an identical product being sold at a premium is aspirin. As Harris and Seldon mention in a footnote, well-advertised aspirin brands sell for several times the amount charged for budget brands, but this is not necessarily proof of consumer irrationality. If people are prepared to pay a few pennies more for the peace of mind that comes from using a drug made by a respected supplier, it is scarcely the worst that can be said of the

---

2 Patent medicines and the outlandish claims made on their behalf cast a long shadow over advertising for years.

advertising industry. It is worth adding that such brand loyalty in that context encourages research and development which otherwise is often encouraged by artificial means such as patents. Besides, it is much more usual to find markets in which products are distinctly different. Entrepreneurs do not launch a new brand in order to provide consumers with a variety of homogeneous goods, but because they believe their brand to be better. It is through innovation that products differentiate themselves and it is advertising that announces these innovations. All of this is to the benefit of consumers. 'Over time little changes in products create major improvements', writes Holcombe (2009: 27), 'and old product characteristics fall by the wayside, replaced by new and improved products, generating economic progress'.

The manipulation of consumers?

If, as many critics argue, advertising is manipulative then what are the tricks used to coerce us? The standard reference here is Vance Packard's *The Hidden Persuaders* (1957), which is routinely cited as an exposé of subliminal advertising. In fact, there are no direct references to subliminal advertising in Packard's book and it is a myth that 'sub-threshold' messages have ever been used in television commercials.[3] When Packard (2007: 31) wrote about the

---

3   There is a nice irony in people reading *The Hidden Persuaders* and thinking that they have seen references to subliminal advertising when they have not.

advertising industry's attempts to 'channel our unthinking habits, our purchasing decisions, and our thought processes by the use of insights gleaned from psychiatry and the social sciences', he was referring to research into the psychological reasons that drove consumers' desires ('depth probing'), not hypnotism.

Advertisers are naturally interested in finding out why people buy certain products. The use of psychological research in advertising was not new in the 1950s (Marshall mentioned it in 1919) and Packard tended to sensationalise the often banal insights provided by 'depth probing'. These findings included the observations that insurance is bought for peace of mind and lingerie is bought to reaffirm a woman's femininity. Packard presciently asked whether 'all this depth manipulation of the psychological variety will seem amusingly old-fashioned' by the year 2000 (Packard 2007: 219). None of this resembles subliminal advertising, i.e. messages entering the subconscious without the conscious mind noticing. To cite Packard's observations as evidence that 'we may have little choice about whether or not we respond to advertising' is quite absurd (Alexander et al. 2011: 41).[4]

For some critics, the mere fact that advertising sometimes increases sales is proof of manipulation. In their

---

4   The report from which this quote is taken seriously suggested that advertising billboards be forced to carry the following disclaimer: 'This advertisement may influence you in ways of which you are not consciously aware. Buying consumer goods is unlikely to improve your wellbeing and borrowing to buy consumer goods may be unwise; debt can enslave' (Alexander et al. 2011: 53).

view, an advertising campaign that shifts goods has made people act in a way in which they otherwise would not have acted and they have therefore been coerced or deceived. This is a zero-sum view of markets in which the advertiser can only win by making the consumer lose. It leaves no room for consumer sovereignty, free will or mutual benefit. No distinction is made between persuasion, the provision of useful information and manipulation.

But, as Mises noted, if advertising could compel people to buy things, business would be about nothing but advertising (Mises 1996: 321). If advertising had the power that its critics attribute to it, companies would use it to drive up aggregate demand when the economy is in decline; in fact, advertising spending and national income tend to be positively correlated (van der Wurff and Bakker 2008; Albert and Reid 2011: 11). Of course, advertising can help sell goods, but the mechanisms are more complicated than critics assume. For example, as Schudson (1993: xv) notes, retailers tend to stock advertised goods and so the mere availability of these goods can lead to more sales. It is quite possible, therefore, that 'advertising helps sell goods even if it never persuades a consumer of anything.'

The social critics make much of the 'lifestyle' aspects of advertising in which marketeers sell mundane products with the promise of a glamorous life. They argue that consumers are duped into buying 'unnecessary' products by advertisements that have little substance and appeal only to our desire for status. It is true that some adverts act in this way (Ferrero Rocher being the classic – though possibly tongue-in-cheek – British example), but this aspect of advertising is greatly exaggerated. If one takes a cool look at the advertising that appears in newspapers and on public transport to see how much of it includes factual information such as price, specifications and how to buy, it is clear that the traditional selling tools of 'features and benefits' remain firmly at the heart of advertising, and 'the most evidently successful advertising is still the advertising that abandons all efforts at psychological manipulation and just tells people that the product offered is on sale or has a low price' (ibid.: 64).

If the purpose of advertising is, as critics claim, to create demand for unnecessary wants, then we are left with the question of why so much money is spent advertising essential goods. Necessities, however narrowly defined, are advertised all the time. Supermarkets advertise food and drink. Estate agents advertise houses. Clothes, shoes, soap, toothpaste, milk, nappies, tampons, washing powder and toilet paper are all promoted in expensive television commercials. If the 'central role of advertising is to create desire where none previously existed' (Berry 2013: 112), it is difficult to explain why so much money is spent marketing goods for which demand is proven and practically universal. The only plausible conclusion is that these advertisements are intended to encourage existing customers to stay with their brand while encouraging customers of rival brands to switch. The toilet paper manufacturer is not advertising in the hope of getting more people to use toilet paper. The toothpaste seller is not trying to initiate the brushing of teeth.

Advertising is overwhelmingly focused on driving 'selective demand' for individual brands rather than driving 'primary demand' for an entire product category. Except in the case of products that are new or obscure, businesses have little interest in building support for a product category. Budweiser does not want you to drink more alcohol, it wants you to drink their alcohol. Temperance campaigners sneer at the notion, but it is a lot easier to get a beer drinker to switch to a different brand than to get a teetotaller or somebody who prefers wine to start drinking lager. It is possible that extensive advertising might help the beer market to grow, but the growth of an entire product category is neither the primary intention nor the likely outcome of the promotion of one brand (in fact, beer consumption has been in decline in Britain for forty years while the market for wine – which is much less advertised – has grown enormously).

The main exception to this rule is when a new product category is created and a company needs to sell an unfamiliar new invention, such as a touchscreen computer tablet or an electronic cigarette. If the existing customer base is small or non-existent, creating demand for the new brand inevitably creates primary demand for the whole category. Furthermore, if there is only one firm in the market initially, creating demand for the category creates demand for the particular company. This type of advertising is mainly informative, (i.e. 'product x is now available and this is what it does...') and it gives a free ride to competitors (if any exist) who benefit from the public being made aware of the new market.

But in the case of universally known products that have been around for years, driving overall demand is improbable without underlying social changes. It is difficult enough to get consumers to change their brand, let alone change their behaviour. Occasional attempts by trade associations to lift demand for entire product categories such as eggs, milk and coffee typically have had little effect (Schudson 1993: 25). Explicit advertising for behavioural change, such as government campaigns to eat 'five a day', abstain from drugs or vote in elections do not lead to conspicuous success.[5] Even the relentlessly partisan British newspaper industry has less effect on people's politics than is often assumed; for example, a third of *Daily Mail* readers voted for Labour or the Liberal Democrats in 2010 despite the newspaper's editorial stance (Ipsos-Mori 2010). Despite all the efforts of business, government and the media, we remain stubbornly resistant to behaviour modification.

Once again, the academic literature supports the view that advertising has little effect on total demand. Indeed, it is more likely that consumption 'causes' advertising than advertising 'causes' consumption (Ashley et al. 1980). Stewart and Kamins (2006: 287) conclude that:

> Both the empirical evidence and logical deduction offer compelling evidence that marketing communication does not create demand; it is a response to demand. People buy things because they want them, not because advertising

---

5   Although some single-issue campaigners portray industry advertising as highly effective in building primary demand, they are generally pessimistic about their own public information films, despite it being only the latter that makes overt calls for behavioural change.

somehow compels them to purchase. When the influence of primary drivers of demand, like demographic changes, broad societal changes, and the effects of other marketing actions, such as lower price, are controlled, there are no studies that demonstrate that marketing communication creates demand for established products.

Faced with this evidence of consumer sovereignty, critics either dismiss it as being so counter-intuitive (to them) that it must be untrue (Hastings 2013: 61) or portray the research as part of a conspiracy among economists to maintain their prestige (Berry 2013: 90).

But the basic point remains. Advertising is not – and cannot be – coercive in any meaningful sense. It can encourage us to try new products and it can inform us about what is available, but there is no mechanism by which reasonably honest advertising can trick or force us to do anything. At worst, it can lodge an annoying jingle in our mind or make us feel a sense of guilt,[6] but the mere fact that a successful advertisement can linger in the memory or generate sales is not evidence of manipulation. It is more likely that critics resort to the accusation of manipulation because it gives them an explanation for why the masses do not share their tastes.

---

6   Charities can be particularly adept at instilling a sense of guilt with campaigns that focus on the plight of the less fortunate.

5 DOES NANNY KNOW BEST?

The root of a lot of the criticisms of advertising is a strong sense of paternalism on behalf of critics and campaigners. Firstly, there are those who believe that advertising creates 'wants' that are not good for the individual or for society as a whole. Secondly, there are single-issue campaigners who often try to use campaigns against advertising as a first step towards trying to get a product itself prohibited. In addition, there has been an increasing literature in recent years that has attacked the very notion of choice.

Social criticisms of advertising

Questions remain about the effects of advertising on profit, pricing and competition, partly because of so-called endogeneity concerns (that is, do large and profitable companies advertise more or does advertising make companies large and profitable?) and partly because some advertising is simply ineffective. However, the general picture is quite clear and the key findings are summarised in the *New Palgrave Dictionary of Economics* (Schmalensee 2008):

> Empirical studies suggest that advertising is not an important determinant of consumer behaviour and that

advertising follows rather than leads cultural trends. On the core issue of whether advertising is anti- or pro-competitive, the evidence suggests that advertising is associated with lower prices.

Faced with decades of empirical evidence, advertising's critics have switched their attention from its economic effects to its allegedly malign social effects. From Arnold Toynbee saying in the 1960s that he 'cannot think of any circumstances in which advertising would not be an evil' to the 2011 anti-advertising tract entitled 'Think of Me as Evil?', there is a deep moral opposition to advertising that cannot be tackled with evidence alone.

The standard social criticism draws heavily on the theory of manipulation outlined in the previous section. It claims that advertising works by 'enticing people to buy things that they neither want nor need' (Korten 2001: 269). But what are wants and what are needs, and does it matter? In his famous essay 'Economic Possibilities for our Grandchildren', John Maynard Keynes drew a distinction between 'those needs which are absolute in the sense that we feel them whatever the situation of our fellow human beings' and 'those which are relative only in that their satisfaction lifts us above, makes us feel superior to, our fellows' (Keynes 2009: 197). Demand for needs, he argued, was finite and was close to being satiated when he was writing in 1930. Demand for wants, however, was almost infinite. Despite his stated belief that the desire for wants 'may indeed be insatiable', Keynes nevertheless assumed that both needs and wants would be satisfied within a century and that people would then choose leisure over material goods. This led him to predict that we would one day choose to work only fifteen hours a week. 'Keynes clearly believed,' writes Berry (2013: 89), 'as a good middle class English liberal, that once freed, most people would give up the senseless pursuit of status-driven consumption in order to develop the higher sensibilities and refinements of Bloomsbury.'

History has so far shown Keynes to have been wrong about our latent desire for leisure. But why is this? In *The Affluent Society*, published in 1958, J. K. Galbraith blamed advertising for driving demand for 'unnecessary' consumer goods and thereby compelling people to work longer hours than they otherwise would. Like Keynes, he drew a distinction between wants and needs, asserting that the only legitimate production in an industrial society is that which meets the demand for mankind's 'urgent wants'. The wants of an individual, he claimed, are fixed and innate. If the desire for a product is artificially created by the industry that profits from its sale, then the desire is inauthentic and the resulting demand is false (Galbraith 1999: 124):

> If the individual's wants are to be urgent, they must be original with him. They cannot be urgent if they must be contrived for him. And, above all, they must not be contrived by the process of production by which they are satisfied. For this means that the whole case for the urgency of production, based on the urgency of wants, falls to the ground. One cannot defend production as satisfying wants if the production creates the wants.

Even if we accept Galbraith's self-imposed rules about what is and is not an 'urgent want', proponents of free markets do not justify capitalist production on the grounds that all needs are as urgent as hunger. On the contrary, a large part of the case for a free economy is that it raises living standards far beyond subsistence living. Enabling people to spend an ever-smaller proportion of their income on bare necessities is a benefit, not a problem, of the free market. If advertising plays a part in lifting the aspirations of mankind, then it is all the better for it. Advertising can be justified on the basis that it encourages people to buy products that were once seen as luxuries. As Harris and Seldon argue in *Advertising in a Free Society*, 'advertising cannot be judged by whether it enables man to satisfy existing wants more effectively; it must be judged by its ability to create (or crystallise) new wants.'

Galbraith and Keynes present us with a false dichotomy when they talk about wants and needs. They depict 'needs' as the handful of goods and services needed to sustain life while dismissing everything else as unnecessary 'wants'. Both assume that we should prefer unnecessary leisure to unnecessary goods. Keynes asserts that we buy non-essentials purely in order to feel superior to our peers while Galbraith asserts that anything we buy after seeing an advertisement brings us no benefits. Neither acknowledges the vast middle ground between bare necessities and status symbols which is filled with goods and services that we do not need to survive but which are nevertheless useful or enjoyable.

It is true that economists tend not to make a distinction between the relative importance of products when discussing supply and demand. Common sense tells us that the most 'urgent' needs of food, housing, clothing and heating will be met first and that disposable income will be spent on non-essentials. As disposable incomes grow, the range of non-essentials that can be profitably advertised expands. Economic growth leaves people with more money to spend and companies use advertising to fight for custom. Galbraith, however, sees reverse causation at work. In his view, people would not spend their money in the absence of advertising, except on a select group of 'urgent' needs. 'If production is to increase,' he writes, 'the wants must be effectively contrived. In the absence of contrivance, the increase would not occur.'

In sum, these contrived wants (Galbraith calls them 'demons') serve no purpose and therefore the products themselves, together with the industries that make them and the advertising that promotes them, also serve no purpose. Their utility is zero, a point made explicitly by Galbraith (1999: 131) and by his intellectual descendants (Capra and Henderson 2009: 5):

> Since human needs are finite, but human greed is not, economic growth can usually be maintained through the artificial creation of needs through advertising. The goods that are produced and sold in this way are often unneeded, and therefore are essentially waste.

It takes a peculiar view of mankind to view the desire for better living standards as 'greed' and to classify every product except those that are needed for physiological survival as 'waste'. To illustrate how incoherent this view is, it is worth considering an example. Is a washing machine a want or a need? Given that it releases time that would otherwise be spent washing clothes, perhaps even Keynes would be confused by this. If having a washing machine is not an artificially created want, is it desirable for machines to be developed that use less energy, are more reliable, use less water, clean clothes better, do not shrink woollen clothes and are less likely to catch fire? A similar argument could be made in relation to cars. Are safer cars, cars that need fewer oil changes and fewer services wants or needs? Perhaps Galbraith would argue that any form of car is a want and not a need. But, then, what about trains, buses and bicycles? The reality is that all goods and services fulfil desires. We may demand some goods and services more than others at a given level of income and the demand for different goods and services will be satiated at different rates as we consume more of them.

Nevertheless, from these assumptions the social critics draw two conclusions. Firstly, that the consumer is, contrary to the mainstream economic view, not sovereign because his desires are contrived for him by commercial interests. Secondly, that the consumer should settle for less or, as Galbraith put it, should ask himself 'if the solution lays with more goods or fewer demons.'

Galbraith's argument rests on a form of naturalistic fallacy which gives more weight to innate desires than to those which are created by exposing individuals to wider possibilities. Like some of the earlier critics (for example, Braithwaite 1928), he assumes that an individual's pre-advertising preferences are his 'true' – and, by implication, optimal – preferences. But if, as most economists believe, advertising provides information, this suggests that the preferences of the ignorant are more legitimate than those of the informed, and, since his definition of innate needs is so narrow, the logical conclusion of his argument is that people would be happy – perhaps happier – living in the most spartan conditions were it not for advertising.

Harris and Seldon regarded all of this as condescending nonsense. They were appalled that 'moralists', 'aesthetes' and 'arrogant autocrats' scoffed at the working man's 'striving for better material conditions of life'. They were clearly surprised that 'a reputable economist [Galbraith] has seriously argued that the age of affluence has arrived'. Of course scarcity is a relative concept, they said. Scarcity is 'a necessary accompaniment of a progressive society. It could be abolished tomorrow if the peoples of the world suddenly became satisfied with their lot. If scarcity vanished, so also would ambition and striving for improvement.'

It is trivially true to say that needs are, by definition, more urgent than wants, but this does not mean that satisfying wants is unimportant or undesirable. In a 1961 essay written in response to Galbraith, Friedrich Hayek pointed out that the same logic would render all art and literature redundant. 'The innate wants are probably confined to food, shelter, and sex', he wrote. 'All the rest we learn to desire because we see others enjoying various things. To say that a desire is not important because it is not innate is to say that the whole cultural achievement of man is not important' (Hayek 1961).

To caricature the Galbraithian social criticism only slightly, it is that manufacturers devise pointless new products which advertisers then trick us into buying. With the exception of a handful of enlightened intellectuals, consumers never notice that they are the victims of a gigantic deception and never understand that their living standards are not, contrary to all appearances, improving. Yet there is a wealth of evidence to show that advertising cannot sell a bad product, that advertising tends to follow social trends rather than create demand, that the majority of new products fail (with or without advertising), that consumers are rarely fooled twice, that most advertising is ignored or derided, and that 'advertising is not an important determinant of consumer behaviour' (Schmalensee 2008).

Nevertheless, the belief that it is the advertiser, rather than the consumer, who is sovereign was common in the 1950s and it remains common today. It was an important theme in such as books as David Potter's *People of Plenty* (1954) and Vance Packard's *The Hidden Persuaders* (1957) and *The Status Seekers* (1959), as well as later tracts such as David Korten's *When Corporations Rule the World* (1995), Oliver James's *Affluenza* (2007), Robert and Edward Skidelsky's *How Much Is Enough?* (2012) and Gerard Hastings's *The Marketing Matrix* (2013).

Why is this view so prevalent on the political left? Hayek believed that socialists' rejection of the fruits of economic growth was the result of them losing the battle for production (Hayek 1961):

> For over a hundred years we have been exhorted to embrace socialism because it would give us more goods. Since it has so lamentably failed to achieve this where

it has been tried, we are now urged to adopt it because more goods after all are not important. The aim is still progressively to increase the share of the resources whose use is determined by political authority and the coercion of any dissenting minority. It is not surprising, therefore, that Professor Galbraith's thesis has been most enthusiastically received by the intellectuals of the British Labour Party, where his influence bids fair to displace that of the late Lord Keynes.

But Hayek also observed that Galbraith's ideas had found support among some Conservatives:

It is more curious that in this country it is not recognized as an outright socialist argument and often seems to appeal to people on the opposite end of the political spectrum. But this is probably only another instance of the familiar fact that on these matters the extremes frequently meet.

This meeting of minds between left-wing and right-wing critics continues today. Religious leaders and environmental activists have also entered the fray. Archbishops and aristocrats echo the same arguments against advertising as eco-warriors and Marxist professors. Their motives may differ, with the 'aristocratic objection' against mass produced ugliness (Schudson 1993: 256) contrasting with the new left's complaint that materialism has become the people's opiate, but the song remains the same.

Objections to advertising made by 'those who object to the intrusion of commerce into their comfortable lives', as Harris and Seldon put it, smack of elitism and snobbery. For the most part, the social critics of advertising are – to quote Kirkpatrick (1994: 71) – 'thinly disguised elitists who cannot tolerate the fact that advertising, marketing, and capitalism very rapidly turn the expensive toys of the select few into everyday comforts of the masses'. The message that underlies the argument about 'wants' and 'needs' is that the masses should be given what they need, not what they want. As the alleged creator of new desires, advertising takes the blame for people buying goods and services that intellectuals avoid. Mises put it succinctly in 1949: 'Like all things designed to suit the taste of the masses, advertising is repellent to people of delicate feeling' (Mises 1996: 320).

Advertising and single issue campaigners

One common argument made against advertising today was considered by Harris and Seldon too silly to address in detail. The idea that the government should ban advertising on paternalistic or moral grounds is dismissed in *Advertising in a Free Society* in a single paragraph:

> Because advertisements are used to sell almost every conceivable product and service, they offer a large target for those whose real objection is to the thing advertised. People who disapprove of betting, smoking, drinking, hire purchase, self-medication, birth control, Roman Catholicism or 'Billy Graham' campaigns, all find advertisements to condemn; and they are joined by those who object to the intrusion of commerce into their comfortable lives. No doubt advertising mirrors the imperfections of human society, but we shall not waste much time on critics who aim at the reflected image instead of declaring

openly against smoking or gambling or hire purchase or whatever it is they dislike. While the law permits such activities, their advertising must be tolerated.

The observation that those who would prohibit advertising for certain products are attacking the 'reflected image' of their enemy is a shrewd one. The real aim of such campaigners is usually to suppress the product entirely, starting with its most visible face on billboards and television. Just as those who oppose capitalism fight a proxy war against advertising, single-issue campaigners oppose advertising as a substitute for attacking the product and its consumers directly.

Advertising, smoking, drinking and public health

The ostensible justification for banning advertisements for disfavoured products is that fewer people will consume them as a result. Harris and Seldon clearly believed that this was none of the government's business and, as we have seen, the effect of advertising on primary demand is often negligible anyway. Single-issue campaigners who support product-specific advertising bans rely on the questionable beliefs of the 'social critics' – that consumer sovereignty is a myth; that advertising is coercive; and that advertising creates, rather than follows, demand. These beliefs are held in the field of public health to a much greater extent than they were in the 1950s. The hapless consumer is portrayed as being inescapably drawn to ruinous habits by advertising. From this, it is a short step to portraying advertising almost as murderous and its prohibition akin to wiping out a disease. Hastings (2013b), for example, asserts that 'alcohol problems are driven by marketing just as surely as malaria is driven by the mosquito'.

Does alcohol advertising 'cause' underage drinking? Does gambling advertising 'cause' problem gambling? Does tobacco advertising 'compel' people to start smoking? Here, the economic literature conflicts with the claims made by campaigners. The economic studies tend to show that the advertising of alcohol and tobacco has the same effect on overall demand as most advertising for established products: little or none (Nelson 2006). Qi (2008: 6) notes that 'almost all surveyed studies found no significant effects of [tobacco] advertising on aggregate demand'. Similarly, Duffy (1995: 557) concludes:

> In an empirical application to data for the alcoholic drinks and tobacco markets in the United Kingdom, it is concluded that aggregate advertising appears to have had little or no effect upon product demand in this sector over the past three decades.

Evidence from jurisdictions that have banned the advertising of certain products supports these conclusions. Alcohol advertising bans do not reduce consumption (Nelson 2010) and it is doubtful that adolescents are influenced by them (Strickland 1985). Single-issue campaigners sometimes claim that those who are 'exposed' to alcohol advertising in their early years are more likely to start drinking at a younger age and/or become heavier consumers in adulthood. Similar claims are made about 'junk food' and smoking, all based on survey data, but their proponents have failed to give a satisfactory answer to the obvious question of whether frequent consumers recall more advertising because they are more interested in the product rather than becoming interested in the product because of advertising (Chen 2005; Schudson 1993: xvi).

The most famous natural experiment is the US's broadcast ban on cigarette advertising in 1971, which led to 'vast savings in total industry advertising, but no changes in industry sales' (Qi 2013). Advertising spend fell by 25 per cent immediately after the ban was enacted, but prices remained the same, profits rose and the tobacco industry oligopoly was protected from serious competition. In other words, the ban resulted in the same anti-competitive outcomes that have been observed when the advertising of any product has been banned or restricted but it did not reduce demand (Eckard 1991). If cigarette advertising bans reduce sales at all, it is through the indirect process of raising barriers to entry, thus allowing incumbent companies to set higher prices than would otherwise be the case (Tremblay and Tremblay 1999).

Despite the negligible effect of such prohibitions, Berridge (2013: 151) notes that health campaigners often attribute the ubiquity of cigarette smoking in the twentieth century to mass marketing. 'This type of argument is powerful', she writes, 'and has been much used also by public health advocates in their later campaigns for the restriction and banning of advertising. It argues for the "duping" of consumers, and tends to see them as passive recipients of advertising messages.' However, as historians have long recognised, large-scale advertising of cigarettes began only after the product had a significant customer base and was clearly in the ascendancy (Berridge 2013: 152; Tinkler 2006: 271). Although the rise of cigarette smoking among women in the inter-war years is often attributed to clever marketing – most famously, Edward Bernays's 'torches of freedom' stunt in 1929, which portrayed the freedom to smoke as a feminist issue – there was no cigarette advertising aimed at women until the late 1920s in the US. Far from initiating female smoking, tobacco companies nervously refrained from making explicit overtures to women until social attitudes had changed and the habit had become common. 'It is more accurate to observe that cigarette smoking among women led tobacco companies to advertise toward the female market than to suggest that advertising created the market in the first place' (Schudson 1993: 183).

Campaigners react to the economic evidence in disbelief. 'Why,' they ask, 'would companies spend so much money on these advertisements if they didn't work?' The mistake in this line of reasoning is to project their own beliefs about the purpose of advertising onto the advertisers. From their perspective, advertising for 'unhealthy' products is intended to recruit underage consumers and promote excessive consumption. But if the advertiser has the same intentions as other businesses (to keep its own customers while encouraging others to switch) it is wise for them to continue advertising. Indeed, so long as its rivals advertise, it would be commercial suicide to do otherwise.

The 'tyranny' of choice

Perhaps the most peculiar modern criticism of advertising is that it creates too much choice. Barry Schwartz begins his book *The Paradox of Choice* with a personal anecdote about buying a pair of jeans in the 1990s. Wanting 'regular jeans', he is 'stunned' to be offered a range of slim fit, relaxed fit, baggy, extra baggy and other variations. This seemingly mundane retail scenario had a profound effect on Schwartz's outlook (Schwartz 2004: 1–2):

> By creating all these options, the store undoubtedly had done a favour for customers with varied tastes and body types. However, by vastly expanding the range of choices, they had also created a new problem that needed to be solved. Before these options were available, a buyer like myself had to settle for an imperfect fit, but at least purchasing jeans was a five-minute affair. Now it was a complex decision in which I was forced to invest time, energy, and no small amount of self-doubt, anxiety, and dread.

Similarly, Gerard Hastings's anti-advertising polemic *The Marketing Matrix* includes the following passage (under the heading 'Happy in our servitude') (Hastings 2013: 37):

> A standard supermarket in the wealthy developed countries will offer us 40,000 different products [...] This pandering to whims we didn't even know we had is turning us into hoity-toity prigs who must have things just-so. A British public that discovered wine little more than a generation ago, now demands specific grape varieties as a matter of course; where once black tea would suffice we now have endless variations on the theme (loose

leaf, tea bags in numerous shapes and materials, varying strengths, different blends) as well as green tea, white tea and countless types of infusion.

The short response to this is that supermarkets do not carry a wide range of products on their shelves to taunt us, confuse us or waste our time but because people have different preferences. Some people might be happy with a plain white loaf, but there are enough people who want a panini or baguette to make it worthwhile stocking them.

Yearning for the era of getting what you are given is not a serious critique of the mass market. Those who are struck by 'anxiety' and 'dread' when confronted with consumer choice should console themselves with the fact that the comforting but limited range of products available in the 1940s are mostly still available and can be easily found without examining all 40,000 products in the supermarket. Indeed, if time is really the issue when faced with so much choice, one can always choose products at random.

Truth in advertising

Much of the criticism of advertising stems from the fact that the whole advertising business does not work in the way that outsiders intuitively assume it must. They find it incomprehensible that companies would spend money on advertising if they did not make a greater return through increased sales resulting from higher demand. But while that is sometimes the case, it is not that simple. In his critical assessment, *Advertising: The Uneasy Persuasion*, Michael Schudson explains that consumer goods advertising works, but that it 'does not work the way the lay person generally assumes'. He continues (Schudson 1993: 42–43):

> Advertisers use advertising as one way of coping with the ever uncertain world of changeable consumers and wily competitors, but they hedge the bets they place on it. They put advertising money behind products with already demonstrated popularity. They direct advertisements to populations already using the same or similar products, already known to have large disposable incomes, and often already known to be heavy users of the advertised good [...] If, normally, businesses expect advertising to be but one marketing tool among many and if they generally hope that it will help redistribute consumers of a given product category among the brands of that category rather than shifting consumers' buying patterns towards a new range of products, then it is difficult to argue that advertising is a prime mover in directly creating a culture of consumption.

It is difficult not to conclude that the critics of advertising take the whole subject too seriously. In essence, advertising is no more than the 'art of making known' (Schwarzkopf 2009: 7). It is information from a biased source, regulated to prevent outright deception (Kirkpatrick 1994: 29):

> There is nothing mysterious or incomprehensible about the way advertising works. In content, an advertisement says only one of three things (sometimes two or three of these in combination). In introductory campaigns, the ad says, 'New product for sale.' In competitive campaigns, the ad says, 'Our product is better than the competition's.' In reminder campaigns, it says, 'We're still here, don't forget us.' That is all.

Many of the world's largest corporations spend only around two per cent of their revenue on advertisements (Laya 2011) and while advertising remains the most efficient way for a company to communicate with its customers in a mass market, its social and economic importance is much exaggerated. The *New Palgrave Dictionary of Economics* notes that advertising has been 'controversial, probably more than its economic importance would justify' (Schmalensee 2008). The economist Julian Simon, having researched the issue in depth, concluded that 'the economic study of advertising is not deserving of great attention', ruefully adding that 'this is not a congenial point at which to arrive after spending several years working on the subject' (Simon 1970: 284–85).

Harris and Seldon observed that many critics of advertising 'seem to have lost their sense of humour about persuasive appeals that exploit vanity and selfishness and shamefully contain no details of chemical or technical performance. The ordinary shopper has kept his head much better.' Many of the critics appear to have a low opinion of the public, whom they assume will buy whatever is put in front of them regardless of quality. But, as Harris and Seldon remark:

> [they] have ignored the part played by the fish queue, the pub, the child welfare clinic, the morning train – in fact, the power of consumers to defend themselves by swapping information and experience – in keeping markets competitive and traders and suppliers up to the mark. The sovereignty of the consumer is much greater than many economists who have never understood the market system have supposed.

When pressed, even the staunchest opponents of advertising and consumerism concede that people are not easily taken in by the marketers. At the end of Vance Packard's *Hidden Persuaders* comes the admission that in 'virtually all situations we still have the choice, and we cannot be too seriously manipulated if we know what is going on' (2007: 239). In *Luxury Fever*, Robert H. Frank (1999: 174) notes:

> since advertising hyperbole is common knowledge even among children, most of us discount advertising claims, and it thus seems unlikely that even fledgling consumers are seriously misled.

In *Affluenza*, Oliver James concedes that 'from as long ago as the 1930s in America, the great majority of the population have believed that advertising is misleading' (2007: 232). Michael Schudson, one of advertising's more thoughtful critics, notes that it 'is part of popular culture that advertisements are silly [...] people ignore the vast amount of advertising they see and distrust much of the little advertising they take in' (Schudson 1993: 227, 252). As long ago as 1759, we find Dr Samuel Johnson observing that 'advertisements are now so very numerous that they are very negligently perused'.

Why, then, does advertising receive such a bad press from so many? 'Perhaps', mused Harris and Seldon, 'the reason for their cussedness is that they do not share the basic belief in a free society.' This brings us to the heart of the matter. If advertising is 'capitalism's way of saying "I love you" to itself' (Schudson 1993: 232) then crusading against advertising is a way of registering your hatred of capitalism. The socialist historian Robert McChesney makes this explicit, saying: 'Advertising is the voice of capital. We need to do whatever we can to limit capitalist propaganda, regulate it, minimize it, and perhaps even eliminate it' (Mirrlees 2009). Similarly, the left-wing academic Gerard Hastings complains that advertising provides 'the mask that gives capitalism its acceptable face' (Hastings 2013: 14).

Many attacks on advertising act as a proxy for a war on capitalism and consumerism, but if the critics are against economic growth, they should say so openly.[1] Some critics claim to have environmental objections, arguing that advertising leads to consumption and that consumption leads to environmental destruction. Leaving aside the empirically dubious basis for these claims, those whose real concern is pollution should pursue environmental objectives directly. Tackling resource depletion and pollution by clamping down on advertising is like tackling drink-driving by taxing petrol.

Whatever influence the advertising industry may or may not have over us, it can do no more than attempt to persuade. For rhetorical reasons, critics like to refer to this persuasion as 'manipulation', but it is no more manipulation than their own attempts to persuade us of their rightness of their cause. Galbraith himself was in the persuasion

---

1   Some do. Gerard Hastings, for example, writes: 'We need to give our leaders permission to act. To reassure them that we understand that going backwards on material wellbeing is an acceptable and necessary price to pay if we are going to make progress on much more meaningful forms of wellbeing' (Hastings 2013: 150).

business and those who disagree with his view of the good society may regard his books – for which, incidentally, nobody has an innate 'need' – to be as socially undesirable as some find advertising. No reasonable person would call for his books to be burned, however, and the same regard for free speech should be afforded to advertisers.

Commercial speech is not held in such high regard as academic speech, but it should be defended. The freedom of businesses to inform and remind the public about their wares has generally been a blessing to consumers. It has kept markets competitive, improved efficiency and lowered prices. It subsidises the press to such an extent that some newspapers can be given away for free. It reduces the cost of tube and bus tickets, pays for countless Internet services, gives us dozens of television channels and numerous radio stations. Globally, it provides billions of pounds in sponsorship for sports, arts, music and cultural events.

The coercive effect of advertising is almost entirely imaginary, but the coercion involved in its prohibition, in part or in whole, is very real. Let the buyer beware, by all means, but let him also be aware of the many benefits of open communication between buyer and seller in the free market.

REFERENCES

Albert, A. and Reid, B. (2011) The contribution of the advertising industry to the UK economy. The Work Foundation.

Alemson, M. A. (1970) Advertising and the nature of competition in oligopoly over time: a case study. *Economic Journal* 80: 282–306.

Alexander, J., Crompton, T. and Shrubsole, G. (2011) Think of me as evil? Opening the ethical debates in advertising. Public Interest Research Centre/WWF-UK.

Armentano, D. (1999) *Antitrust: The Case for Repeal*. Auburn: Ludwig von Mises Institute.

Ashley, R., Granger, C. W. J. and Schmalensee, R. (1980) Advertising and aggregate consumption: an analysis of causality. *Econometrica* 48(5): 1149–67.

Ayanian, R. (1975) Advertising and rate of return. *Journal of Law and Economics* 18: 479–506.

Bagwell, K. (2007) *The Economic Analysis of Advertising*. Handbook of Industrial Organisation, Elsevier.

Benham, L. (1972) The effects of advertising on the price of eye-glasses. *Journal of Law and Economics* 15: 337–52.

Berridge, V. (2013) *Demons: Our Changing Attitudes to Alcohol, Tobacco, and Drugs*. Oxford University Press.

Berry, M. (2013) *The Affluent Society Revisited*. Oxford University Press.

Bloch, H. (1974) Advertising and profitability: a reappraisal. *Journal of Political Economy* 82: 267–86.

Braithwaite, D. (1928) The economic effects of advertisement. *Economic Journal* 38: 16–37.

Cady, J. F. (1976) An estimate of the price effects of restrictions on drug price advertising. *Economic Inquiry* 14: 493–510.

Capra, F. and Henderson, H. (2009) Qualitative growth. Institute of Chartered Accountants of England and Wales, October.

Chen, M., Grube, J., Bersamin, M., Waiters, E. and Keefe, D. (2005) Alcohol advertising: what makes it attractive to youth? *Journal of Health Communications* 10: 553–65.

Clark, C. R. (2007) Advertising competition and competition in the children's breakfast cereal industry. *Journal of Law and Economics* 50(4): 757–80.

Comanor, W. S. and Wilson, T. A. (1967) Advertising, market structure and performance. *Review of Economics and Statistics* 49: 423–40.

Comanor, W. S. and Wilson, T. A. (1974) *Advertising and Market Power.* Cambridge, MA: Harvard University Press.

Duffy, M. (1995) Advertising in demand system for alcoholic drinks and tobacco: a comparative study. *Journal of Policy Modelling* 17(6): 557–77.

Eckard, E. (1991) Competition and the cigarette TV advertising ban. *Economic Inquiry* 29(1): 119–33.

Economist, The (2001) Who's wearing the trousers? 6 September.

Frank, R. H. (1999) *Luxury Fever.* New York: The Free Press.

Galbraith, J. K. (1999) *The Affluent Society.* London: Penguin.

Greenslade, R. (2013) NUJ calls for public subsidies to save newspapers from closure. *Guardian*, 6 November.

Hastings, G. (2013) *The Marketing Matrix: How the Corporation Gets Its Power – And How We Can Reclaim It.* London: Routledge.

Hastings, G. (2013b) Marketing to kill for. Presentation at Balance North East Alcohol Summit, 22 November.

Hayek, F. (1961) The non sequitur of the 'dependence effect'. *Southern Economic Journal* 27(4): 346.

Holcombe, R. G. (2009) Product differentiation and economic progress. *Quarterly Journal of Austrian Economics* 12(1): 17–35.

Ipsos-Mori (2010) Voting by newspaper readership 1992–2010.

James, O. (2007) *Affluenza.* London: Vermilion.

Kaldor, N. (1950) The economics of advertising. *Review of Economic Studies* 18: 1–27.

Keegan, V. (2007) Will Myspace ever lose its monopoly? *The Guardian*, 8 February.

Keynes, J. M. (2009) *Essays in Persuasion.* New York: Classic House.

Kirkpatrick, J. (1994) *In Defence of Advertising.* Claremont, CA: TLJ Books.

Kirzner, I. (1971) Advertising: speech at the Foundation for Economic Education. 5 August.

Klein, N. (2000) *No Logo.* London: Flamingo

Korten, D. (2001) *When Corporations Rule the World.* Bloomfield, IN: Kumarian Press.

Kwoka, J. E., Jr (1984) Advertising and the price and quality of optometric services. *American Economic Review* 74: 211–16.

Laya, P. (2011) Do you pay enough for advertising? One big corporation spent a jaw-dropping $4.2 billion last year. *Business Insider*, 6 June.

Lippmann, W. (1914) *Drift and Mastery: An Attempt to Diagnose the Current Unrest.* New York: Mitchell Kennerley.

Love, J. and Stephen, F. (1996) Advertising, price and quality in self-regulating professions: a survey. *International Journal of the Economics of Business* 3(2): 227–48.

Marshall, A. (1919) *Industry and Trade.* London: Macmillan.

Miller, M. C. (2007) Introduction to *Hidden Persuaders* (in Packard 2007). Brooklyn: Pocket Books.

Milyo, J. and Waldfogel, J. (1999) The effect of price advertising on prices: evidence in the wake of 44 Liquormart. *American Economic Review* 89: 1081–96.

Mirrlees, T. (2009) Media capitalism, the state and 21st century media democracy struggles: an interview with Robert McChesney. The Bullet Socialist Project, 9 August.

Mises, L. von (1996) *Human Action: A Treatise on Economics.* San Francisco: Fox and Wilkes.

Murphy, R. (2011) *The Courageous State.* London: Searching Finance.

Nelson, J. (2006) Cigarette advertising regulation: a meta-analysis. *International Review of Law and Economics* 26(3): 195–226.

Nelson, J. (2010) Alcohol advertising bans, consumption and control policies in seventeen OECD countries, 1975–2000. *Applied Economics* 42(7): 870–926.

Ogilvy, D. (2007) *Ogilvy on Advertising.* London: Prion.

Packard, V. (2007) *The Hidden Persuaders.* New York: Ig Publishing.

Qi, S. (2013) The impact of advertising regulation on industry: the cigarette advertising ban of 1971. *Rand Journal of Economics* 44(2): 215–48.

Schmalensee, R. (2008) Advertising. In *New Palgrave Dictionary of Economics* (2nd edn), ed. S. Durlauf and L. Blume. Palgrave Macmillan.

Schudson, M. (1993) *Advertising, The Uneasy Persuasion: Its Dubious Impact on Society.* New York: Basic Books.

Schwartz, B. (2004) *The Paradox of Choice.* New York: Harper Collins.

Schwarzkopf, S. (2009) What was advertising? The invention, rise, demise, and disappearance of advertising concepts in nineteenth- and twentieth-century Europe and America. *Business and Economic History Online* 7.

Simon, J. (1970) *Issues in the Economics of Advertising.* Urbana, IL: University of Illinois.

Stewart, D. and Kamins, M. (2006) Marketing communications. In *Handbook of Marketing* (ed. B. Weitz and R. Wensley). London: Sage.

Strickland, D. E. (1982) Alcohol Advertising: orientations and influence. *Journal of Advertising* 1: 307–19.

Sweney, M. (2012) Louise Mensch calls for subsidies for local newspapers. *Guardian*, 25 April.

Telser, L. G. (1964) Advertising and competition. *Journal of Political Economy* 72: 537–62.

Thomas, L. A. (1999) Incumbent firms' response to entry: price, advertising and new product introduction. *International Journal of Industrial Organization* 17: 527–55.

Tinkler, P. (2006) *Smoke Signals: Women, Smoking and Visual Culture in Britain.* Oxford: Berg.

Tremblay, A. and Tremblay, V. (1999) Re-interpreting the effect of an advertising ban on cigarette smoking. *International Journal of Advertising* 18: 41–49.

Tungate, M. (2007) *Ad Land: A Global History of Advertising*. London: Kogan Page.

Weiss, L. W. (1969) Advertising, profits, and corporate taxes. *Review of Economics and Statistics* 51: 421–30.

Whyte, J. (2007) Spread the word about the benefits of advertising. *Financial Times*, 26 June.

Wurff, R. van der and Bakker, P. (2008) Economic growth and advertising expenditures in different media in different countries. *Journal of Media Economics* 21: 28–52.

PART 2

ADVERTISING IN A FREE SOCIETY: THE CONDENSED VERSION

RALPH HARRIS AND ARTHUR SELDON

ABOUT THE CONDENSED VERSION

This edition of *Advertising in a Free Society* has been edited down from 100,000 to 30,000 words. Harris and Seldon included many sets of figures which time has rendered redundant, along with a number of case studies of such products as Double Diamond beer and Toni perms, which are of only tangential interest to the modern reader. Discussions about such issues as retail price maintenance are no longer major political talking points and have been excluded. Instead, we reproduce the meat of Harris and Seldon's arguments with some abridgements. All footnotes are from the original unless stated otherwise.

Advertising in a Free Society originally contained fourteen appendices of which six have been included here, two in edited form. The first takes detergent advertising as a case study. Harris and Seldon echo the widely held scepticism about the 'white lies' of washing powder manufacturers, all of whom claim to make laundry whiter and brighter than their competitors. The 'large claims, the pseudo-scientific evidence, and the extravagant language' of this (then) relatively new industry allow the authors to study advertising at its worst and yet, despite a tendency towards oligopoly which may or may not have been driven by intensive advertising, Harris and Seldon find that consumers have been well served by lower prices and vigorous competition.

The second appendix is a brief discussion of subliminal advertising, a topic that evidently caused concern after the publication of Vance Packard's *Hidden Persuaders*. As Harris and Seldon note, no serious evidence of subliminal advertising had ever been produced and yet this 'persistent myth' (Miller 2007: 13) has not entirely faded from sight after half a century.[1]

The third appendix discusses the world of political advertising which Harris and Seldon, like Ogilvy, believed to be the only field of advertising that was systematically and incorrigibly dishonest. They need only to reproduce various political advertising slogans verbatim to illustrate this.

The fourth appendix is a short excerpt from a longer chapter that discussed the likely effect of taxing advertising and subsidising the press with taxpayers' money. Advertising's critics continue to suggest taxation as a vaguely Pigovian response to the supposedly polluting effects of Madison Avenue. As newspaper sales continue to tumble, calls for state subsidies have reared their head once more (see, for example, Sweney 2012; Greenslade 2013).[2] Anyone

---

1 In 1983, David Ogilvy confirmed that subliminal advertising 'did not exist', but confessed to once hiring a hypnotist to help him produce a 30 second commercial. The resulting advertisement was so powerful, he said, that he 'burned it, and never told my client how close I had come to landing him in a national scandal' (Ogilvy 2007: 209).

2 Murphy (2011: 287–88) advocates a tax on advertising that he accepts will threaten the viability of newspapers. However, he recommends the tax revenue be used to subsidise the press 'but only if it agrees to act with political impartiality in the way that the BBC is obliged to do.' This might save some newspapers, but it would hardly leave us with a free press.

familiar with the costs of public notices in local and national newspapers might conclude that the press is already largely subsidised by the taxpayer.

The final two appendices are of mainly historical interest. The first is an account of the extraordinarily inefficient and labour-intensive typesetting practices that were the norm in the British newspaper industry until Rupert Murdoch's dispute with the print unions in the 1980s led to the end of such practices. The second is a reminder of the force of opposition to the creation of commercial television when ITV began broadcasting in 1955.

WHAT THEY HAVE SAID

'Good wine needs no bush.'

—Proverb

'If you wish in the world to advance,
Your merits you're bound to enhance,
You must stir it and stump it, and blow your own trumpet,
Or, trust me, you haven't a chance.'

—W. S. Gilbert

'Advertising is an evil service.'

—Aneurin Bevan

'Advertising is really a form of education.'

—King George VI

'Advertising agents top the list of those who misuse the language on purpose, but it is their job to excite our emotions and atrophy our thoughts.'

—Sir Ernest Gowers

'In an advertisement it is allowed of every man to speak well of himself.'

—Dr Johnson

'Probably half of every advertising appropriation is wasted, but nobody knows which half.'

—Lord Leverhulme

'The advertising quack who wearies with tales of countless cures,
His teeth I've enacted shall all be extracted by terrified amateurs.'
—W. S. Gilbert

'When you advertise you are like a man going bail for his behaviour on his own recognisances for a very substantial sum.'
—Sir Miles Thomas

'Nobody believes the nonsense in any one advertisement.'
—Herbert Agar

'You may advertise a spurious article and induce many people to call and buy it once, but they will gradually denounce you as an imposter.'
—Phineas T. Barnum

'[...] the seller advertises because he thinks that it is the cheapest means of selling his goods. It seems likely that... he is not mistaken.'
—Margaret Hall

'[...] most competitive advertising is a costly extravagance.'
—Samuel Courtauld

'If I didn't advertise I should have to treble my travellers. It would cost just as much and would be a lot more trouble.'
—Lord Mackintosh

'No one pays to advertise his products in order to establish the eternal verities. All advertising is persuasive in intent.'
—Margaret Hall

'Advertising nourishes the consuming power of men. It creates wants for a better standard of living [...] It spurs individual exertion and greater production.'

—Winston Churchill

'A monopoly is created in so far as advertising convinces the customer that no substitute exists.'

—Labour Party

'Unless our freedom of choice is to be a mockery, all novelties must up to a certain point be actually forced on our attention. This means advertising.'

—Sidney Webb

'[...] much advertising by manufacturers is wasteful [because] it is false or misleading [or] because buyers and sellers already know the facts.'

—Professor Arthur Lewis

'Waste is an image that shocks a utilitarian or a Fabian temper, but just as Parliamentary disorder and slowness is often the price of political liberty, so waste is the price of free consumer choice.'

—Daniel Bell

'Even when all our various manufactories have become public services [...] we can easily imagine the various public health departments advertising their baths [...] the educational authorities importuning every young man and maiden to try their attractive lecture courses and organised games [...]'

—Sidney Webb

'If the public lose their confidence and faith in advertising, we are all sunk.'

—Lord Mackintosh

'If a man write a better book, preach a better sermon, or make a better mousetrap than his neighbour, tho' he build his house in the woods, the world will make a beaten path to his door.'

—Emerson

'The tragedy of the working man is the poverty of his desires.'

—John Burns

'We want the tastes of our workers, collective farmers and toilers to develop so that they should pass from simple foods to superior and more nourishing foods. For this purpose we must adopt all forms of propaganda, including the best kinds of advertising.'

—Commissar of Food (Moscow 1951)

ORIGINAL ACKNOWLEDGEMENT

This acknowledgement appeared in the 1959 edition of *Advertising in a Free Society.*

We were helped by the cordial co-operation of the three leading organisations: the Incorporated Society of British Advertisers, the Institute of Practitioners in Advertising, and the Advertising Association. Their Directors, respectively Commander D. C. Kinloch, J. P. O'Connor and L. E. Room, provided papers, suggested avenues of enquiry, and discussed many aspects of advertising about which laymen are largely ignorant. The American Association of Advertising Agencies also provided much useful material.

There are not many economist writers on advertising whom we found directly helpful: with rare exceptions, the academic economists have evolved theoretical patterns that do not help to reveal the role of advertising in the real world, and the few economists inside advertising are not usually able to write freely. We have derived much indirect assistance and stimulation from the teachings of Professors F. H. Knight, W. H. Hutt, Sir Arnold Plant, Lionel Robbins and Sir Dennis Robertson. We wish to acknowledge the advice received from Mr. Basil Yamey who read some of the chapters in draft and offered most valuable comments. For inspiration and insight into the fundamental truths of economics and political philosophy we turned to the classical economists, whose teachings we believe have much relevance to our day.

Finally, we are indebted to the Institute of Economic Affairs, which made this study possible. Like the individuals, organisations and companies mentioned above, it bears no responsibility for our statements of fact nor for our judgements and conclusions.

INTRODUCTION

Advertising has provoked many weighty criticisms but on closer examination most appear to be based on personal, partial or perfectionist standards. Few critics have attempted a balanced assessment. For the purpose of practical policy, it is essential that due weight be given to the economic functions of advertising in our modern complex society. Hence a chief concern of this study is to examine its effectiveness as an aid in promoting the best use of limited resources from the standpoint of the consumer, and, on a longer view, in strengthening or weakening the forces making for economic advance.

Beyond question there are many cases where advertising has been skillfully used to help market goods and services more efficiently than would otherwise have been possible, but it is equally clear that not all advertisements have proved 'productive'. Neither has all research, nor the whole of any other branch of human endeavour. Like the critics, the defenders of advertising make a mistake if they claim too much.

Since most advertising still takes the form of written messages in newspapers, it may be likened to the technique of journalism.[1] Reports and editorials, like the

---

1   Editor's note: this is no longer the case. Newspaper advertising has fallen behind internet and television advertising.

neighbouring advertisements, may not attract the reader's attention; or, if they do, they may not carry conviction. Both can be used to promote false standards, to mislead the public and to encourage behaviour that can be condemned as anti-social. In journalism, abuses are used as arguments not for abolition but rather for vigilance, legal and voluntary restraints and, above all, because the 'truth' is often in keen dispute, for plenty of diversity in the channels of publication.

This tolerant judgement arises from the acceptance of a free press as an integral part of a political democracy. Because rival journalists and newspapers perform their task better than any practicable alternative, constructive critics focus on ways of checking excesses without curtailing the substance of free expression. Might not a similar approach be appropriate in the debate on advertising? As F. P. Bishop has argued: 'If advertising is a necessary part of the economic system, then the social problems it raises are analogous to the social problems associated with coal-mining or the aggregation of large numbers of people in large towns [...] They cannot be used as arguments for abolishing advertising' (Hale 1944).

The neglect of advertising by professional economists suggests that humility would be more becoming than the hostility with which many have frequently approached the subject. It is as a contribution towards remedying this neglect that the present volume is offered.

1   THE NEED FOR ADVERTISING

In earlier ages when men were forced to supply their needs from the direct labour of their families, organised advertising played no part in the economy of strictly local communities. However defined, advertisements consist basically of invitations to buy or sell, to borrow or lend, to work or to patronise worthy causes. Every advertisement is a call to action of some kind or another. It makes no sense unless addressed to people with freedom to decide for themselves the pattern of their work and lives.

But until individual enterprise broke through the ancient bonds of law and custom, the greater part of mankind was not free to choose where to work. Whilst modes of life were, for the majority, ruled by the mediaeval compulsion of status, society was static and living standards stood still. Even after the enclosure of land loosened the chains which for centuries had shackled all but the privileged to the grindstone of subsistence farming, opportunities remained limited. Effective freedom of choice for consumers was confined to the narrow number of alternatives available from itinerant pedlars and occasional fairs. So far as choice of work was concerned, the freedom of contract lauded by the philosophers of seventeenth- and eighteenth-century Britain, mocked a growing army of landless labourers without much prospect of work away from the changing countryside.

Meanwhile in London and other towns the wealthy were escaping from the fixed mould of traditional consumption, and the trader who catered for their indulgences was no longer content to display his wares and shout their merits in the market place. The earliest advertisements took the form of notices about books, theatres, lotteries, wigs, medical remedies, and servants, as well as guidance about property, ships, coaches, schools and charities. There was a growing volume of the lost and found type of advertisement, which, to judge from the papyri in the Cairo museum, is among the most ancient of all forms of public announcements. This assortment of advice, appeal and exhortation was carried in ephemeral news sheets, by specially printed leaflets, or announced from the walls of buildings and even from walking boards, later christened 'sandwichmen' by Charles Dickens.

As foreign trade added to the variety of commerce, advertisers began to offer such luxuries as tea, coffee, spices, silks, silverware, perfumes, cosmetics and slaves. But although Dr Johnson could write in 1759 that 'advertisements are now so very numerous that they are very negligently perused' it was not until a century later that many were addressed to a wider audience than the most prosperous inhabitants of a few large cities.

Gradually foreign trade broadened men's vision beyond the horizon of national self-sufficiency. Apart from introducing strange merchandise, it brought to Britain new skills and rival religions. It increased knowledge and helped to create a ferment of ideas from which emerged the liberal philosophy of free trade between countries endowed with differing natural resources. Finally, international commerce led to the accumulation of wealth in the hands of capitalists who were well placed to take the lead in financing the earliest workshops and mines of the industrial revolution.

Costs of marketing

So long as each local community supplied most of its own requirements, buyers and sellers were known personally to one another or would meet naturally in the market place. The demand for various foods, clothing and equipment would remain stable over long periods and would be regularly matched by established suppliers. Producers, having one foot in the market, were able to cater for the particular needs of their customers.

This became impossible as the scale of production increased. If the manufacturer were to keep his factory running so as to make the best use of his specialised men and machines, he was driven to tap wider circles of custom and maintain a regular flow of trade outwards to ever more distant markets. To bridge the growing distance to his scattered customers, the producer had to store goods, locate markets (or employ middlemen for this purpose), transport supplies in bulk, and ensure their distribution in a form suitable to the final consumer.

Because these costs of marketing often increase rapidly as the scale of output expands, some critics have argued that they represent a wasteful dissipation of the economies reaped in production. This is a short step removed from the view that the expenses of attributing a commodity are in some way artificial, or at any rate less essential than those incurred in its production. But, as Alfred Marshall pointed out, there is no analytical basis for any such distinction: 'The sailor or railwayman who carries the coal above the ground produces it just as much as the miner who carries it underground; the dealer in fish helps to move on the fish from where it is of comparatively little use to where it is of greater use, and the fisherman does no more'. Marshall conceded that there might be too many traders (as there might be too many workers employed in a factory), but he suggested that, instead of reviving mediaeval attacks on trade, writers should attack 'the imperfect organisation of trade, particularly of retail trade'.

In principle the labourer and the trader are equally productive. Neither can create products out of nothing: both work on their respective materials to adapt them better to the satisfaction of the consumer. Production and distribution are no more than two phases in the supply of a commodity, whose price will properly reflect all the costs incurred up to the point of purchase.

Nevertheless, Marshall allowed that with modern methods of manufacture a conflict inevitably arose between the costs incurred under these two headings. The very process of large-scale production which yielded great savings in unit costs created an enlarged supply of goods that could be brought to market only with increasing difficulty. Distribution costs must therefore offset, in some degree, the economies reaped by mass production. It was upon this very fact that Marshall relied for his exposition of competitive equilibrium in industry. If there were no marketing problem, a few large firms would grow to dominate the industry. Increasing returns would enable the giants to destroy their smaller rivals, and the theory of competition would be exposed as an absurd abstraction in a world of potential monopolists. In practice, market penetration involved heavy expenses which checked the cost-reducing tendencies of large-scale production.

Wide and accessible markets existed for a relatively small number of uniform commodities, such as raw materials (cotton, wheat, iron, and so on) or what Marshall called 'plain and common' products (steel rails, calico, and so on), and in these cases the economies of large-scale production were exhausted long before any single supplier grew big enough to claim a significant fraction of the total market. For the rest, Marshall argued that marketing costs would impose an earlier check on growth, preventing any firm from exploiting to the full the possible economies of mass production. He offered various explanations why this check would operate with different products: 'some of them aim at creating a new want, or at meeting an old want in a new way. Some of them are adapted to special tastes and can never have a very large market, and some have merits that are not easily tested and must win their way to general favour slowly'.

Marshall concluded this part of his argument by posing the very dilemma which most advertisers deliberately set out to solve: 'In all such cases the sales of each business

are limited [...] to the particular market which it has slowly and expensively acquired; and though the production
itself might be economically increased very fast, the sale
could not'.

The mass market

At the time Marshall was writing, towards the end of the
nineteenth century, the unreality of assuming fixed wants
was being demonstrated by the dynamic course of events.
When a trade journal reported that 'the grocer had been up
to 1846 at any rate [...] the minister of luxuries to the rich',
the date chosen as the watershed was the beginning of the
great era of free trade. Once the untramelled division of labour could be applied between countries, as well as within
callings, there followed a vast expansion in the volume and
variety of merchandise, matched by a rapid growth in the
purchasing power of the masses. Household consumption
of tea, sugar, meat, bacon and other foods increased rapidly, despite the unparalleled rise in population. More and
improved clothing, furniture and domestic supplies came
within reach of growing numbers of families.

From higher wages, families had money to spare for
other than basic physical necessities, and during the second half of the nineteenth century a growing number of
new products began competing for a place in the mass
market. Processed foods such as condensed milk, cocoa,
meat extracts and margarine appeared alongside choco-
lates and sweets marked with the name of national suppliers such as Cadbury, Fry and Maynard. By the 1870s

and 1880s new inventions brought forth the early models of sewing machines, typewriters, cycles, cameras, piano players, stoves, baths and lavatories. To begin with, most manufacturers set about marketing their wares by employing travellers to call upon retailers, wholesalers and, in some cases, potential customers in their own homes. But this often proved a laborious and costly method, and, outside the food and clothing trades, wholesalers frequently proved an unsuitable channel for distributing a rapidly growing assortment of keenly competitive products. To win access to the developing mass market, manufacturers could establish their own outlets for selling directly to the public, set up their own wholesaling organisation, or alternatively they could advertise over the heads of retailer and wholesaler in the effort to stimulate public demand for their goods through the existing trade channels. Examples of the first method during the closing decades of the century were seen in chemists' goods (Boot's, Timothy White's), groceries (Lipton's, Home & Colonial, Maypole, Pearks), sweets (Maynard's), footwear (Freeman, Hardy & Willis) and in beer with the extension of tied houses. Some enterprises, like the Co-operatives and, later, Marks & Spencer, which started as multiple retailers to the mass market, either developed their own manufacturing subsidiaries or contracted with independent manufacturers to supply merchandise to their specifications.

The alternative method of marketing products by mass advertising had long been pioneered by suppliers of proprietary medicines; indeed, it was the reluctance to be allied with 'quacks' that deterred many manufacturers from making use of this technique. Among the first to prove the value of national advertising were Hudson's, Pears' and Lever's in the rapidly expanding soap business. Lipton's, Pearks and others had also begun to advertise their low-price chain stores. What helped to encourage others to start advertising was partly the pressure of competition, but perhaps even more decisively the availability of an expanding medium for national advertising in the form of popular newspapers and magazines eager to sell 'space'.

A national press

When, in 1712, a tax of one shilling was imposed on published advertisements, the politicians were deliberately aiming to curb the growth of an independent press. The fact that this was swiftly followed by many failures, including that of *The Spectator*, proves that, despite limited circulation and high prices, papers had already come to rely upon advertising as a source of revenue. At that time, according to Francis Williams (1957), of the nine daily papers circulating in London five were 'primarily advertising sheets' whilst the remainder devoted at least half their space to advertising. For well over a century the advertising tax, on top of paper and stamp duties, made it almost impossible to maintain a regular newspaper by the revenue from sales alone. When *The Times* was established in 1785 it relied, like most other serious papers of the period, upon a direct subsidy from the politicians.

From his perceptive study of newspaper history, Francis Williams concludes that 'the daily press would never have come into existence as a force in public and social life if it had not been for the need of men of commerce to advertise. Only through the growth of advertising did the press achieve independence'.

The advertising tax, which had been raised to 3s 6d in 1803 and reduced to 1s 6d in 1833, was finally abolished in 1853. The loss to the Budget of approaching £200,000 showed that proprietors had been able to sell an impressive amount of space to financial advertisers, book publishers, the sellers of cures and curiosities, as well as for personal announcements, legal and official notices. Shortly afterwards, the stamp duty and paper tax were also swept away, and the 640 papers of 1855 grew to above 3,000 by the end of the century. Prices dropped, circulations moved steadily upwards, and new papers were launched, starting in the 1850s with the *Daily News* and the *Daily Telegraph*, both sold for the unheard of price of one penny. With the spread of universal education after 1870, magazines such as *Tit Bits*, *Answers*, and *Pearson's* were established to cater for popular tastes; and in 1896 Alfred Harmsworth started the *Daily Mail*, which sold at a half-penny and achieved a sale verging on one million, four years later.

Because advertising was the chief source of revenue for the cheap press, the bid for circulation took the form of competitions, prizes, gifts and every kind of promotion, including outright advertising by the papers themselves. It was these developments which presented advertisers with most difficult questions of choice between alternative papers, questions which were solved only by the growth of specialised advertising agencies to advise them on how best to employ newspapers, posters, circulars and other media to deliver their sales 'message' to the audience they wished to reach. In more recent years the best agencies have made efforts to reduce wasteful advertising expenditure by measuring circulations, estimating markets, testing appeals and other techniques still being developed.

But in the years before 1914, when mass advertising was still largely confined to the more adventurous or aggressive companies, hit-or-miss methods allowed far greater scope for costly failures as well as for outstanding success where a manufacturer possessed a natural flair for this new form of 'salesmanship in print'.

Branded goods

It was the development of a national network for press and poster advertising that enabled manufacturers to launch their branded products into widening markets. This has led some economists to blame advertising for 'product differentiation' and to hark back to a regime of 'pure competition'. The ideal of a perfect market with a homogeneous product traded by numerous suppliers none of which could get more than the ruling price was contrasted with an 'imperfect' market broken up into spheres of influence, each dominated by a large-scale producer selling an exclusive brand at an allegedly arbitrary price.

Leaving aside the economic analysis of this criticism, we must briefly examine its historical validity. It is true that, apart perhaps from patent medicines, tobacco and soap, nationally known brands were not very important until the later decades of the nineteenth century. It is also true that, with the help of advertising, branded goods have invaded one field after another until they now cover large sections of food, clothing, furniture, electrical and other consumer goods. But it is not true that an orderly and efficient system of competition had prevailed before the advent of mass advertising. Even when trade was still confined to simple agricultural produce, difficulties of transport and communication prevented the establishment of wide, open markets in which a single price ruled for uniform products, irrespective of the particular supplier. As consumers came to buy foods which had undergone grading, blending or some other process of preparation (at first performed by the retailer), there was a further departure from product homogeneity.

For manufactured goods, innovation in technical and marketing methods leads to product differentiation. From the days of mediaeval guilds, craftsmen made a practice of fixing their name or mark to their own product, as much from a feeling of pride as from the acceptance of responsibility to the purchaser. Yet the craftsman was well-known personally to his local patrons. As the distance between producer and consumer widened, the brand-name (or some other evidence of origin) provided a convenient bridge between them. For the producer it was a way of building up goodwill and establishing a more dependable market for the products of his fixed plant and equipment. For customers, the brand enabled them to buy again those things which had previously given satisfaction as well as to avoid wasting more money on those which did not. In fact, as Professor Sir Arnold Plant (1937) has pointed out, branding is essentially a grading device which helps the public to identify a particular product and to associate it with an expected quality, taste or other standard of performance.

Revolution in retailing

The national advertising of branded goods directly to the final customer accelerated changes in the pattern of retail distribution. We have seen that the early shops had sprung up to cater primarily for the convenience of the monied minority. Their pace was leisurely; elaborate service was the essence of their personal relationship and customers were charged accordingly. For most consumer goods there was nothing approaching a national market but a series of local outlets, insulated by barriers of distance, prejudice, tradition and ignorance. Similar products sold for different prices, depending on the source of supply, the individual customer's willingness to pay, and the type of shop through which it was processed and prepared for sale.

It was neither the shopkeepers themselves nor even the advertisers who started the movement towards more efficient methods of retailing which spread swiftly during the later decades of the last century. As Mr Basil Yamey (1954a,b) has pointed out, the initiative came from new classes of customers, seeking better outlets for their growing purchasing power.

More enterprising retailers were quick to take advantage of wider public demand for less elaborate service and keener prices. The more successful began to expand their scale of operation, either by adding to the range of merchandise stocked or by building up chains of shops served by highly efficient purchasing and importing specialists. As a result, in Mr Yamey's judgement: 'By the end of the century the department stores, multiples and vigorous small or medium scale private traders had displaced the co-operative societies as the pacemakers of change and of competition in the retail trades.'

This streamlining of retail trade was helped by the spread of advertised, branded and packaged merchandise which not only speeded the turnover of stocks but also made for easier handling by less skilled shop assistants, so that grocers, for example, could sell cigarettes, confectionery and patent medicines.

Inevitably there were protests from traders' associations against this disturbing trend towards what amounted to pre-selling goods over the retailer's head and so facilitating price-cutting among them. Grocers complained about the threat to their traditional skills and, even more vociferously, about competitive methods which offered the public lower prices to compensate for less service. Starting with books, chemists' goods, tobacco and certain groceries, retail associations began to insist that manufacturers enforce fixed resale prices which would afford acceptable profit margins, secure from the inroads of would-be 'price-cutters'. Those manufacturers with an established brand were at first reluctant to deny their ultimate customers the benefit of lower prices, especially as their advertising helped retailers sell more of their goods with less effort. But, to hard-pressed traders, any form of overt competition spelled risks they were not prepared to accept, so they responded by discriminating against manufacturers who refused to enforce fixed prices, endeavouring instead to push the sales of rival suppliers who 'played the game' on resale price maintenance.

In this way, since the 1890s more and more manufacturers have been reluctant parties to trade restrictions which have prevented the public reaping part of the potential economies which advertising makes possible, although owing to the inflated number of shops which price maintenance has attracted beneath its umbrella, it is by no means clear that the enemies of competition have gained from their early victories.[1]

Early examples and excesses

Prominent amongst the companies which, before 1914, were described as having been 'built by advertising' were medicine vendors and soap makers. Health and cleanliness could be sold to everyone, and, while low unit prices carried these products within reach of the mass market, repeat sales in millions of homes brought large profits which afforded the resources for lavish advertising campaigns.

Patent medicines, in particular, lent themselves to sensational advertising methods. The more alarming the disease, the more loudly 'cures' were promised, and even

1 More shopkeepers may have been kept in business but their average income has not risen in line with those from other occupations.

allowing for the backward state of medical knowledge only the ignorant (or ill) could have regarded many of the claims as other than frivolous and fanciful. Of 'Professor' Thomas Holloway's universal ointment (on which over £30,000 was being spent in 1855), *Punch* wrote: 'it will mend the legs of men and tables equally well and will be found an excellent article for frying fish in'. The success of these early quacks set the stage for an era of unrestrained competition in which the growing power of press and posters was exploited by many advertisers for their own ends. A barely literate public was expected to be on its guard against false pretences; caveat emptor was the ruling doctrine and the customer might secure redress in the courts only when an advertiser was so incautious as to go beyond vague promises and offer a 'guarantee' which lawyers might accept as a part of the contract of sale. While Thomas Beecham was content to recommend his pills as being 'worth a guinea a box', less scrupulous rivals made outrageous attacks on doctors and played on the public's fear of serious diseases. It was the British Medical Association which provoked a government enquiry into such abuses and led to the establishment of voluntary and legislative checks.

The fourfold increase in the sale of soap during the fifty years following the repeal of the duty in 1853 owed a great deal to W. H. Lever (the first Lord Leverhulme), who graduated from his father's grocery business in Lancashire to become the leading manufacturer of soap in Britain. Like Pears' and Hudson's, Lever's Sunlight soap was at first recommended on its own merits with the promise of domestic cleanliness and easier washing days. The very success of these companies attracted a multitude of small producers who found that soap of a sort could be made quite simply and supplied in anonymous yellow bars for grocers to sell to an undiscriminating public. Such competition drove the leading companies to use fiercer methods of promotion and more aggressive advertising, which insisted on the superior merits of their own brand of soap and cast doubts on the value of all rival products. To facilitate identification, Lever decided to sell his soap in packets, and, to encourage 'brand loyalty', offered prizes based on the collection of wrappers. By the 1890s more than £100,000 a year was being spent on promoting Lever's and Pears' soap, and the proprietor of Pears (Thomas Barratt, who unsuccessfully sought to advertise on postage stamps) claimed that, as a result, soap was transformed in quality and greatly reduced in price. The soap war abated only with the amalgamation of the leading companies before 1919.

Cigarette and tobacco companies were using cards, albums and other prizes to advertise their rival brands before the end of the nineteenth century. But the really spectacular period of cigarette advertising occurred in 1901, when a concerted attack on the British market was threatened by the American Tobacco Company. The British companies fought back, using posters, press and gift schemes. Godfrey Phillips, having been refused all eight pages of a London paper in return for 'a fabulous sum', made do with four pages which he used to attack foreign goods (especially those of 'Yankee trusts') and urge the public to buy its own British cigarettes (then selling at five for one penny). Stability came in December when the Imperial Tobacco Company was formed by a dozen rival firms which retained a large measure of autonomy in marketing their separate brands.

Consumer durables provided early proof of the serious use of advertising in building up demand for such new products as sewing machines, typewriters, cameras, bicycles and motor cars. When in 1905 Ingersoll advertised his five-shilling watch, jewellers were not enthusiastic about stocking such a cheap line until advertising began to tap fresh layers of customers. When, in 1905, Gillette brought his first safety razor to Britain it cost one guinea. Advertising, employed to overcome public prejudice against all such novelties, had the effect of extending sales, stimulating competition and reducing prices.

By 1914, advertising had come to embrace a great diversity of activities, some of the highest value to the developing British economy, much of indifferent value to any but the promoters, and some positively harmful to the public as well as obstructive to a competitive economy. Newer advertisers embarking on a serious selling operation had no doubts that advertising would be of greater value if the abuses of quacks and mountebanks could be stopped. Nor was it only from other advertisers that abuses came. Media owners were not always scrupulous in their efforts to cash in on this lucrative business. The next fifty years witnessed continuing efforts to eliminate abuses, improve standards and to raise the sights as well as the efficiency of advertising. From adolescence, advertising has struggled against many temptations towards maturity.

Advertising arrives

Writing of the period before 1914, an advertising man admitted (Milne 1956): 'It was a time when much roguery was rampant, when advertising operated under what one might call frontier conditions'. A director of the Incorporated Society of British Advertisers likewise castigated some of the early pioneers for producing advertisements that were 'crude, meretricious, vulgar and dishonest'. The trouble was that whilst advertising remained 'a comparatively new and undisciplined business, it attracted too many of the wrong kind of people'. More specifically, he lamented that 'parasites and tricksters gravitated to it', while thoughtful people regarded advertising as at best repugnant, and at worst a racket.

None of this should surprise us. By 1900 advertising was a lucrative and growing field. While its principles and practice remained uncharted it was bound to attract people whose intentions were not always honourable. Anyone could set up as an advertising agent; training, qualifications and codes of conduct were unheard of; advertisers lacked experience, and every phase of their business lacked method and measurement; and just as the claims made in advertisements lacked moderation, their presentation lacked artistry. At a time when many people could barely read or write, and before modern techniques of typography and blockmaking had been developed, advertisements relied for their attraction on tricks and sensationalism.[2]

---

2   When in 1886, the Millais painting 'Bubbles' had been used to advertise Pears' Soap, there was an outcry against the prostitution

Until the mid twentieth century, spending money on advertisements and judging the result depended on the crudest guesswork. Neither data nor statistical tools existed to measure press circulation, readership, buying habits, market penetration and other records of systematic selling. Few advertisers thought of integrating their advertising campaigns into a comprehensive marketing strategy, designed to suit the product, its price, packaging, sales force, customers and retail outlets. Advertising was regarded by most early practitioners as little more than conjuring with persuasive slogans and attacking rival products without much concern for truth or taste. If, after decades of continuing improvement, most laymen remain ignorant of the great advance in standards, efficiency and honesty, the blame lies mainly with organised advertising which has so far neither publicised its impressive progress, nor made available to serious students the information on which a more just appreciation could be based. The rest of the blame is on the shoulders of those advertisers who, out of carelessness or contempt for the public, still fall short of the standards accepted by the majority.

Whatever today's critics may think about the prevalence of false and misleading advertisements, there can be no doubt that standards have improved enormously. Whatever further improvements may be possible by these

---

of art. Since then many eminent artists, including Graham Sutherland, have been pleased to earn fees by preparing advertisements. From the field of literature, Agatha Christie, J. B. Priestley and W. H. Auden have written copy for advertisers, as Lamb and Byron are reputed to have done.

and other methods, those who appreciate the almost limitless extent and diversity of advertising in a free society will also understand that its regulation – without undue encroachment upon individual liberty and responsibility – poses a constant challenge to all the interests concerned.

2   THE CRITICS

We are chiefly concerned here with the criticisms of advertising made by economists because they ask the right questions even if they have not always provided the right answers. The other criticisms worthy of consideration – aesthetic, ethical, political – also come out in their analyses, and are further discussed in later chapters.

The classical economists showed little interest in advertising because, although in use for two centuries or more, it did not play a major role in the early industrial economy before the middle of the nineteenth century. The economists who followed them were not much interested in it either because, in its extravagant exuberance, much of it looked rather a joke. Also, apart from its support for newspapers, it appeared to have little economic significance in the production and distribution of goods and services.

Large-scale advertising of goods in wide demand grew rapidly towards the end of the nineteenth century and Alfred Marshall, whose writings unite the nineteenth and twentieth centuries, was the first major economist to take much notice of advertising as a subject for economic analysis. He distinguished between 'constructive' advertising, designed to inform people about products offered for sale, which he thought was beneficial, and 'combative' advertising, which was primarily not informative but repetitive, and which was wasteful, even if it raised output and lowered cost, because such economies could have been reaped without advertising (Marshall 1919).

The classical critics

Marshall was the first of a series of major economist critics of advertising. The second was Professor A. C. Pigou, who drew a broadly comparable distinction between 'informative' and 'competitive' advertising, the purpose of the latter being primarily to divert demand for a commodity from one firm to another (Pigou 1920). Most advertising, he thought, was competitive and therefore undesirable. Advertising could lead to arrangements between formerly independent firms and therefore to monopoly; it could be abortive, the advertising efforts of competing firms cancelling one another out; and it could merely substitute the products of one firm for those of another and more efficient firm. On the whole, Professor Pigou thought advertising was wasteful, and that the waste might be prevented by taxing or even prohibiting 'competitive' advertising.

Mrs D. Braithwaite[1] considered the distinction between informative and other advertising logical but impracticable, although she judged that most was not informative. She thought that if it increased output by facilitating standardisation and mass production, and reduced costs

1 In an article on advertising in *The Distribution of Consumable Goods*, 1932.

per unit and therefore prices, it was beneficial. On the other hand, if it merely redistributed the demand for different commodities, resources were used in a less desirable pattern from the community's point of view.

Advertising could also restrict competition because price and quality lost their power as instruments of competition and were replaced by the power of producers to win markets by creating 'reputation'. The process of creating 'reputation monopolies' was cumulative and a vicious advertising circle was set in motion.

Professor E. H. Chamberlin (1935) and Mrs Joan Robinson (1933) are conveniently considered together because their original analyses were in some respects similar. They developed Mrs Braithwaite's notion of reputation monopolies by claiming that advertising could be used to 'differentiate' products from one another by emphasising the less important advantages and so create loyalty for each brand; this gave each advertiser a pocket of monopoly and he could then charge a higher price for his product and earn a higher profit, but his output was lower than it would be under perfect competition.

A. S. J. Baster (1935, 1947) mounts a formidable offensive against 'the wastes involved in building up brand-names and reputations by competitive advertising'. He argued:

> [T]he most outrageous deceptions can be practised on the long-suffering public for an indefinite time before they are found out, and in consequence an unnecessarily large part of the production machine is turned over to the making of things that sell well in place of others, equally desired, which do not.

For much of this he blames the educational system for producing people ready 'to waste their substance on goods and/or activities they would avoid if they knew the facts'. And so:

> One of the most depressing consequences is the development of successful advertising techniques based on the principle that so long as adult consumers can be got to recognise a brand name on a packet, the less they know about the contents that has any relation to its merits, the more they will buy it.

The left-wing critics

Professor W. A. Lewis adapts the older economists' distinction between informative and combative advertising to the two classes of retailers' and manufacturers' advertising respectively. He argues that consumers are better guided by retailers into buying (standardised or mass-produced) goods they have chosen on the basis of their expert knowledge and experience than by manufacturers each of whom is intent on pushing his own brand or variety on uninformed purchasers. 'It should not be on the manufacturers' strident claims that the public has to rely for information [...] much advertising by manufacturers is wasteful [because] it is false or misleading [or] because buyers and sellers already know the facts.'

The most formidable economic critique of advertising in recent years has come from Nicholas Kaldor (1950). He also accepts the view (which we reject below) that the primary (he calls it the 'direct') function of advertising is to provide information, but argues that it does not do so efficiently. He gives three reasons. The first is that it is both subsidised (by taxation) and also subsidises other services (the press) so that its true cost is not known, and the fact that it is employed does not establish that resources are economically used for supplying it. This is a central criticism and must not be under-estimated. The normal case for supposing that resources are economically used in a free market is that the goods and services they produce would not pay their way unless they satisfied consumer demand; but advertising is not bought separately because it is supplied as part of a commodity or service, and consumers cannot easily evaluate it. Hence, the case for advertising must be made on more complex grounds than merely by appealing to the fact that resources are devoted to it in a free market.

The other two reasons for Kaldor's argument that advertising does not provide information efficiently are that it is biased in favour of the advertiser and that it is costly. On the latter point he claims that advertising cost £68 million in 1938[2] compared with £125 million spent on schools, £87 million on newspapers and periodicals, £10 million on new books, £8 million on universities, £6 million on other research, and £4 million on libraries and museums; and that the information supplied by advertising could be provided more cheaply – for about £14 million – by an independent information service.

---

2   Editor's note: This is the equivalent of £3.9 billion in 2013 prices. In 2013, UK advertising spend was £14 billion. This rise is broadly in line with GDP growth.

But, Kaldor continues, advertising also has 'indirect' effects: it may stimulate the introduction of new products, encourage spending at the expense of saving, and switch demand from some products to others. He argues that the first effect is desirable; the second is desirable in slumps and undesirable in booms, but advertising is not the best way to alter demand and employment; and the third is undesirable. The reasons for his view of the third effect are important because they explain much of what many economists have in mind in their criticisms of advertising; these criticisms have not been fully understood by the advertising profession, nor adequately met.

Retailer domination

The argument is that advertising shifts demand from smaller to larger firms, so reducing the number of firms until the whole output of a commodity is produced by a small number. This is 'oligopoly'. In an oligopolistic market, there is little price competition, because no producer can reduce his price without the others following suit, in which case all would end charging prices too low to make production profitable. So there is often a tacit understanding about prices, and competition takes the form of packaging, samples, coupons, gifts and other attractions that might be considered secondary. The regime of a few large firms brings gains and losses compared with one of a large number of competing middle-sized and small firms. The gains include lower production costs through exploiting the economies of large-scale operation and standardisation, lower capital costs through being able to borrow more cheaply than smaller firms, greater resources from which to finance long-term research, and a greater readiness to embark on risky but nevertheless desirable enterprises. The losses include higher costs of management as organisation becomes complex in larger firms, higher selling costs (including those of advertising), higher prices, barriers to the entry of new firms with new ideas and methods because of the high cost of breaking into the market, and a possibly dangerous concentration of economic power.

This shift towards larger manufacturing units, Kaldor argues, has enabled manufacturers to replace wholesalers and retailers as the dominant element in markets. They have reduced costs, but because competition, the consumers' shield, has been weakened, the reductions have not been passed on to them but have been partly absorbed in selling costs that are higher than they otherwise would be. There is much in the criticisms that cannot be accepted, but some that must be.

The criticism examined: information or persuasion?

The distinction between constructive (or informative) and combative (competitive or persuasive) advertising is based on a misunderstanding of the nature, purpose and rationale of advertising; and the consequent criticism that advertising manipulates demand contrary to the consumer's interest rests on questionable assumptions about the requirements of a free society.

In the first place, the distinction is impossible to draw in practice, and an attempt to assess the amount spent on each of the two kinds would yield bogus results. The mere appearance of an advertisement full of information is itself persuasive; it is not neutral, objective, detached; the information, even if complete and unadorned, is seeking to influence readers in favour of the commodity or service advertised. Even a railway timetable is meant to encourage travelling by train. On the other hand, the most 'persuasive' advertisement contains some information, even if only the name of the product. In fact, all advertising is necessarily both informative and persuasive. Its purpose is – quite properly – persuasive; its method is informative to a greater or lesser degree according to the public to which it is directed and the type of appeal it employs.

Secondly, information is not necessary for an advertisement to have its desired effect. Information may be helpful in advertising a new product. Even then a description may not be as revealing to the consumer as a trial; and an advertisement directing attention to the existence of the new product and inviting the public to buy a trial supply, or perhaps accept a free sample for trial, may be rendering the desirable service even though it contains no word about the product's composition or constituents.

But, for an established product, information may be superfluous. The essential function of advertising is then to remind the consumer of the product's existence. Consumers need reminding because, though spending habits may be strong and change slowly, every day there are new products or services to buy, new incentives to spend money differently.

Brand loyalty is invariably exaggerated by the critics; reminder advertising may be as useful to the consumer as it is essential for the manufacturer. Consumers do not have perfect memories; nor are they a static body: there are continually new potential recruits to be drawn from the newly employed, married or retired, those moving house, and generally from people constantly acquiring fresh interests or needs. Finally, familiar products are, from time to time, improved or adapted to different purposes, and the manufacturer must make this known. Such improvements designed to keep at least one step ahead of the nearest competitor could be confused with the wasteful product differentiation designed merely to distinguish one brand from another.

New wants

Whether advertising is instructive in itself, or not, its effect is informative if it leads people to buy and try a commodity or service they have not known before. In this sense the more persuasive the advertising, the more informative it is. The information comes to the consumer through his experience and trial of the product to which he is introduced; the information is indirect, but it is all the more certain because it is based on use of the product and not on mere description.

This argument is developed by Professor R. H. Coase, who relates it to the theory of consumer choice and demand.[3] He quotes in support Professor F. H. Knight, who

---

3　In an unpublished lecture, 'The Economics of Advertising', delivered at Claremont College, USA, in 1957. We are indebted to Professor Coase for permission to adapt his argument here.

wrote that 'the advertising, puffing or salesmanship, necessary to create a demand for a commodity is causally distinguishable from utility inherent in the commodity itself' (Knight 1921: 339). Moreover, the experience to which even persuasive advertising leads the consumer is not merely the satisfaction of existing wants but of new wants as yet unknown. Professor Knight again:

> The chief thing that the commonsense individual actually wants is not satisfaction for the wants which he has, but more and better wants [...] all intelligently conscious activity is directed forward, onward, upward, indefinitely. Life is not fundamentally a striving for ends, but rather for bases for further striving; desire is more fundamental to conduct than is achievement, or better perhaps, the true achievement is the refinement and elevation of the plane of desire, the cultivation of taste [...] It is not life that man strives for, but a good life [...] For any practical, social purpose, beauty, play, conventionality, and the gratification of all sorts of 'vanities', are more necessary than food and shelter.[4]

In short, advertising cannot be judged by whether it enables man to satisfy existing wants more effectively; it must be judged by its ability to create (or crystallise) new wants. This is its beneficent function, and its service to mankind.

---

4 This view of human choice and desire was not unknown to the older economists. Alfred Marshall said 'although it is man's wants in the earliest stages of his development that give rise to his activities, yet afterwards each new step upwards is to be regarded as the development of new activities giving rise to new wants, rather than of new wants giving rise to new activities.' *Principles of Economics*, 1890.

Furthermore, the consumer may not wish to be bothered with the business of acquiring more information. Broadly, commodities are divisible into those which consumers like to buy after examination and comparison, and those which are bought by repute and name as sufficient evidence of performance or value. This distinction is roughly analogous to that made by economists between 'shopping' goods, for which people like to 'go shopping' and, 'convenience' goods, which are bought usually by name at local shops. For many commodities the consumer wants information, and not merely to enable him to buy wisely but also because shopping and comparing and choosing is a positive pleasure in its own right, a hobby, a fancy, even a fad. Britain abounds in weekend gardeners, 'do-it-yourself' home decorators, car-tinkerers, television-takers-to-pieces, dog-lovers and pig-breeders, who, beginning as amateurs, become more expert than the expert. They insist on information before they buy; and they usually get it: indeed a whole series of periodicals has been developed to serve them.[5]

How much information?

But for other people, or even for the same people when buying other commodities, searching for information would not be a delight but a drudge. And this for good, logical,

---

5 Editor's note: These examples may seem quaint, but the principle still holds (for example with computer-related or mobile-phone-related gadgets).

rational reasons. There is insufficient time to be well-informed in everything: clothes, soaps, pressure cookers, dish-washers, sheets, etc. Leisure comes high in many people's scale of preferences. They are prepared to leave the choice of some products to agents: retailers whose advice and judgement they have learned to respect; or to manufacturers whose brands they have learned to trust. This does not make them the slaves or tools of retailers or manufacturers, for in a competitive economy they retain the ultimate power of veto: they judge not the commodities they buy but their advisers and agents.

It is in this sense that traders and manufacturers properly lay claim to their reputations and standing. They are not will-o-the-wisps, barrow-boys who are here today and gone tomorrow. Their continuing presence is the consumers' guarantee. No shopkeeper or manufacturer would last long if he charged high prices for poor quality – as long as it was exposed to competition.

There is a further point. Some economists have understated the amount of information available to the consumer, and have overstated the degree of 'imperfection' in the market for commodities and services. They have ignored the part played by the fish queue, the pub, the child welfare clinic, the morning train – in fact, the power of consumers to defend themselves by swapping information and experience – in keeping markets competitive and traders and suppliers up to the mark. The sovereignty of the consumer is much greater than many economists who have never understood the market system have supposed.

Also, consumers buy many commodities for their intangible qualities which rationalists may decry but which they are in no position to judge. 'Most goods', says Marghanita Laski (1958), 'are bought, not for what they are, but for what they stand for [...] small wonder then that manufacturers remain almost wholly unmoved by appeals to present their goods to people in a reasonable way, to tell people what their goods are made of, how well they will perform their working function.' But if a bath soap, a pen, or a carpet gives more pleasure when the consumer thinks it is used by a duchess or a television performer, then he is making a logical decision in buying it: he is being more sensible than his critics; and the manufacturer and his advertising agent would be wasting their time and newspaper space in giving information about technical composition or performance. We may think that such irrational grounds for buying are exploited, encouraged and stimulated by sellers and advertising agents, but that is another matter, to which we return below. The point is that in a free society consumers should be free to make their own choices even if they are foolish, provided they are not dangerous. There should be as much information and education and advice and guidance as they are prepared to act on, but the final decision must be theirs. This right and responsibility to make decisions is essential for citizens in a free society. Man develops by making mistakes; the right to buy is a fundamental freedom, even if it carries the risk of buying (harmless) rubbish. And in this sense caveat emptor ('let the buyer beware') does not indicate a primitive condition from which we have moved, but an ideal to which we should aspire. It is implied in the notion of consumer sovereignty as the economic basis of a free society, and it is, in a wider sense, a necessary condition of the political maturity that is the individual's qualification for membership of a free society.

Finally, the critics, including some economists, seem to have lost their sense of humour about persuasive appeals that exploit vanity and selfishness and shamefully contain no details of technical performance. The ordinary shopper has kept his head much better. How often is he fooled? Does he buy a second dose of the rubbish to which he is led by an 'irrational' advertisement? It is the satisfaction derived from the product that brings him back for more. Often it is not so much the advertising that sells the product as the product that carries the advertising. Uninformative but amusing advertising may catch the eye, but it does not sell the goods. Let us not take such advertising so seriously. Standing by itself, it is far less effective than its critics – and perhaps its users – think.

Oligopoly: who dominates whom?

The other major criticisms of advertising concern the supply side of the economic system. They all refer to various ways in which advertising constricts competition and results in making costs and prices higher than they need be. Where objective analysis shows up such dangers, the advertising world must cease scoffing and re-examine their policies. On the other hand, the critics are often guilty of taking too narrow and incomplete a view of the economic system; what they say may be true for short periods, but it overlooks the long-term effect of advertising in attracting competitors, opening the way for innovators, and keeping the economy flexible and dynamic.

Firstly, some economists have gone wrong because they have subconsciously measured the economic system in practice against the models of 'perfect competition' constructed as convenient theoretical devices for teaching purposes. Apart from a few agricultural products which are graded and are sold internationally, such as wheat, 'perfect' competition is a figment of the imagination, although a useful one. In the real world, competition in most industries at any moment is 'imperfect', and advertising may have helped to make it so. But this does not necessarily mean that there has been a fall from grace. If the conditions of demand and supply are such that firms can build 'loyalty' among consumers for their brands in order to reap the economies of large-scale organisation, imperfect competition may be the best situation that is conceivable and practicable. The confusion has been caused by those economists who have given the word 'imperfect' an ethical connotation whereas it has only a strictly technical meaning. It is still true that the less imperfect a market, and the more it approached the 'perfect' model of theory, the better results it might yield in terms of costs and prices. But this is no more than saying that if human nature and technical conditions were simpler we might be better off. That may be: but it is no criticism of economic organisation or of the devices used by producers to enlarge their output. Imperfect competition may be the best possible state of affairs in the economic system. This is true if it has been brought about by the unavoidable causes of human nature and technique; on the other hand, it is not necessarily the best possible condition if it has been brought about by artificial reasons, such as tariffs and an inadequate anti-monopoly law, or positively encouraged by over-generous copyright or patent laws.

To adapt the comment of a candidate for the Premiership about his successful adversary: imperfect competition may be the best competition we can have. It is certainly better than no competition at all; yet some of the critics of imperfect competition write as if no bread would be better than half a loaf. Because competition is imperfect, they argue as though outright monopoly would be better. Perhaps the reason for their cussedness is that they do not share the basic belief in a free society.

This discussion points to a further mitigation of oligopoly. In perfect competition, it is paradoxically possible after a time for one firm or a small number of firms to dominate the market if economies of large-scale production and distribution are such that the large firm is much more efficient and can out-sell the small firm. In time large firms would be challenged by new firms, but for a period they would be supreme. The 'imperfections' which enable small and medium-sized firms to attach customers to themselves enable them to keep going even though they are technically less efficient than the large firms. Imperfections are, therefore, again paradoxically, a means of keeping the market more competitive even in the short run before new ideas and techniques enable newcomers (with the assistance of advertising) to challenge the established large firms.

Long-term competition

Secondly, competition in practice is less imperfect than the critics suppose. Their view is too narrow and too short. It is too narrow because they look at each 'imperfect' or 'monopolistic' competitor or 'oligopolist' separately; they overlook the competition between industries, and they under-estimate the power of potential competition and the dynamic of growth within individual firms in disciplining 'oligopolists' that fail to toe the consumer line.

Each of these errors can be explained briefly. Some of the critics of imperfect competition write as though oligopoly is one degree removed from monopoly. Economists have disputed for many years about the nature of competition between a small number of rival firms, and in particular about the degree of tacit understanding that can be assumed to be taken into account when they decide their trade policies and market strategy. Much of this disputation has been highly tentative and speculative, and very little has been fruitful. But there are plenty of examples in British industry of commodities – soap, detergents, cars, chocolate, breakfast cereals, butter and margarine, radios, petrol, vacuum cleaners, cosmetics, shavers, toothpaste, cigarettes, and many others – that are produced by a handful of firms between which competition is vigorous, although it often takes place in quality or other features rather than in price.

The political parallel is illuminating; it should not be pressed too far, but it helps to dramatise the point. The British 'two-party' system is not merely one degree removed from totalitarianism: it is democracy in action. Under the present electoral system it may not adequately reflect the wide range of opinion among the voters, and there may be dangers of collusion or tacit arrangements to keep out new groups of opinion; but the voter is protected by the possibility or likelihood of disagreement among the handful of existing groups and by the freedom to form new ones. So long as he can cock a snook at the one which power has made unresponsive to his wishes, he is saved from lasting dictatorship, although he may have to suffer it for a while. Political democracy is 'imperfect competition' between oligarchies, but it is worlds removed from one-party dictatorship; economic democracy is imperfect competition between oligopolists, but it is worlds removed from one-firm monopoly.

Moreover, whatever the degree or reality of competition between oligopolists within an industry, they are exposed to the competition of oligopolists in other industries. In the last resort everything competes with everything else for the consumer's attention: one food with another; some foods against drinks; household expenditure against clothes or entertainments or luxuries; spending as a whole against saving. Each industry must watch others that produce alternatives. None can become too autocratic in its business policies without incurring the ultimate sanction of competition: the consumer's cold shoulder. And, as incomes rise, consumers tend to become more fickle and ruthless.

Not least, no oligopolist is safe for all time, nor even is a monopolist. The protection afforded to the railway user by the regulation of railway fares was nothing as compared with the coming of the internal combustion engine and development of the car.

Innovation

Also, the critics of imperfect competition have understated the part played by advertising in maintaining competition and keeping the economy dynamic by facilitating and stimulating the flow of new rivals to challenge established commodities and services. Although it can be, and often is, used defensively to impede innovation, this is the fundamentally beneficent value of advertising from the point of view of the community as a whole, and much more important than its other merits, real or supposed.

The real sources of innovation are deep and complex (see Jewkes et al. 1958). Not that advertising is the only way in which knowledge of new commodities could have been spread: as we emphasise throughout this study, advertising is one of a number of possible methods of marketing a product, and it can justify itself only in so far as it is more efficient than the others are. But, it is undoubtedly one of the most dramatic and rapid ways of spreading information or calling attention to a new product. And, in so doing, it has helped to keep markets competitive, tumbled oligopolists and monopolists, kept prices down, and, in the long run, made the economic system bow to the consumer's will. As Professor Copeland put it: 'The opportunities for keen strategy in the planning of an advertising campaign [...] are one of the mainstays of the competitive system'. And as Professor John Jewkes (1948) wrote:

> [T]he devices by which [...] imperfect competition is brought about - such as advertising - may be the very devices by which the whole system is kept in a dynamic condition. Through them an entrepreneur may take the risk of putting some entirely new product on the market which ultimately proves to be widely acceptable to the public and through which a general sense of buoyancy is created in the economic system. And through them attempts on the part of producers to cash-in on their existing markets secured by advertisement will be frustrated by a crop of new products.

For breaking down the little monopolies which it may create in the short run, for reactivating competition that has become arthritic, we can forgive advertising a lot.

The question remains: what if, as Keynes said, we are all dead in the long run? If the long run consists merely of a succession of short runs, the new competitors who have used advertising to muscle into and break up existing pockets of oligopoly will themselves use advertising to build their own oligopolies, so that over the long run a series of short-lived oligopolists will maintain prices at a higher level than would prevail in a perfectly competitive market. That is true, but again it is inevitable, given human nature and modern productive techniques as we know them. The extent to which greater knowledge and information would break down oligopolies even sooner by reducing the advertising and other costs of breaking into established markets we consider below.

Even admitting its faults, on some of which we have suggestions to make, we do not see that advertising can be dispensed with in a free economy, or even severely inhibited by taxation or state regulation. Unless producers are free to experiment and make mistakes, to 'waste' resources testing the markets for their products (old as well as new), and unless they can use advertising in the process, a free economy is unthinkable. 'Waste is an image that shocks a utilitarian or a Fabian temper, but just as parliamentary disorder is often a price of political liberty, so waste is the price of free consumer choice' (Bell 1956). It is possible to conceive of all kinds of arrangements, such as Kaldor's, in which large retailers inform manufacturers of consumers' requirements, in which advertising can be largely cut out or dispensed with; but they take such a jejune view of human nature that they are hardly worth discussion. Kaldor's 'dominant retailers' have already arrived, and the large retail organisations are often models of efficiency and enterprise; but whether the economy would remain dynamic and progressive if it consisted wholly or even largely of 'dominant retailers' is another question. The economy is now mixed: in some lines the manufacturer is dominant; in others the retailer; and in a few (e.g. textiles, fish, fruit and vegetables, poultry, etc.) the wholesaler is 'dominant', or at least important. There should always remain freedom for the dominance of any type to be challenged; and advertising is one of the most effective instruments by which it can be challenged.

Freedom of choice

Finally, in one respect the critics of advertising openly propose or imply measures that would infringe the principles of the free society. In their vision of manufacturers who do not advertise because retailers tell them what to produce, Lewis and Kaldor envisage a reduction in the variety of products. It would be one thing for consumers, so impressed with the economies of simplification of design and standardisation of quality, size, style, colour, etc., to accept a limitation of choice.[6] But would it stop there? Why should we assume that a regime of retailer dominance would be any more beneficent than a regime of manufacturer dominance? The likelihood is that a limitation on choice, even if it began voluntarily, would harden and become obligatory because it suited the administrative convenience of the distributive machine. Producers, suppliers, traders of any sort are kept in order and have to toe the line because of competition. Remove that and you remove their beneficence. That, in a nutshell, is the case for the free economy that has inspired every liberal economist from Adam Smith to the present day. That is why – with their grasp of human psychology – they have never been so prolific with facile proposals for 'improvements' in economic

---

6 Advertising often encourages such a concentration. For example, an American paper company reduced the number of brands and qualities of toilet tissues from over 2,000 down to two, reducing their cost from 35 cents to 7 cents a roll in a dozen years. Of the $18 million spent on advertising the consumer quite literally paid less than nothing. *Fortune*, November, 1947.

arrangements. It has never been difficult for economists of the other sort to plan to tidy up the system by the simple device of requiring consumers to accept whatever the planners chose to supply.

This study does not take sides for or against any group – manufacturers, wholesalers, or retailers (or any variation or combination of them). Indeed, it is inspired by the belief that in a free society all producer interests should be subservient to the dominance of the consumer. The main essential is that there should be freedom for suppliers (in the light of their greater knowledge of costs) to respond to the preferences of consumers (perhaps in the light of their greater knowledge of commodities). And the only certain guarantee of that freedom is a free economy in an open society.

3   THE CLAIMS

Like the criticisms, the claims for the benefits of advertising we shall consider are mainly the economic ones. There is much confusion about the real issues. We may think that the advertising of some firms beautifies the Underground, is amusing, covers up ugly bomb-sites, makes a cheap press possible, or increases spending and employment. But it is not the function of individual firms to provide public art exhibitions or entertainment, mask the deficiencies of public authorities, 'subsidise' the press, or usurp the economic functions of the government and the banking system. If they spend money to do these things gratuitously they should be accountable to their shareholders but expect no thanks as public benefactors.

The significant economic claims that are made for advertising are mainly three:

1. that it is essential for the development of mass production techniques and for the resulting lower production and/or marketing costs and prices;
2. that it is a guarantee of quality or value, and stimulates product improvement;
3. that it stimulates effort and output by sharpening incentives.

As with the criticisms, some claims are acceptable and others are not. Like the critics, many advertisers and their agents spoil their case by claiming too much. Perhaps even more, advertisers fall down in failing to supply evidence by which their claims might be substantiated.

Reducing costs

Let us first take the claim that advertising increases the scale of production, and therefore reduces costs and prices. It is true that advertising has spread side-by-side with mass production. Two questions must be asked. First-ly, how far is advertising responsible for mass production, i.e. to what extent would mass production not have taken place as extensively or as quickly if there had been no advertising? Secondly, if advertising has accelerated the rate of mass production, is this necessarily a good thing?

There is no lack of examples to suggest that advertising has helped to speed up the growth in the scale of production and so reduce costs. Telling examples include Hoover, Lucozade, Polycell, Toni, detergents, Macleans toothpaste, and others. Such examples could be multiplied a hundredfold.

In 1920 a bull-nosed Morris two-seater sold for £465. When the trade slump came, in January 1921, sales fell from 280 to 74 a month. William Morris cut the price to £375 and increased advertising. Sales rose to 360 in June. Other manufacturers began to cut their prices, and in October Morris reduced his to £299. Sales rose further although total British car production was falling.

Before Lyons' Swiss Rolls were advertised, they sold 10,000 a week at one shilling each. Within a short time after advertising began they were selling 600,000 a week at 8d each.

In January 1922, a 3.5 oz cake of Palmolive Soap sold for 9d. By 1933 increased sales enabled the price to be brought down to 3d, where it stayed until 1940.

Between 1920 and 1938 the sale of Cadbury's half pound blocks and 1d and 2d bars increased nearly five times; the price per pound fell from 4s 4d to 1s 4d.

The cost of brewing Guinness was two and a half times higher in 1954 than 1939, but the selling price, less duty, was only two-thirds higher.

In 1946 a Biro ball-point pen sold for £2 15s; in 1958 there are ball-point pens for as little as one shilling.[1]

How much credit can advertising claim for these impressive results of increased output? Advertising is one method of raising, stimulating or maintaining demand, and it is one among several: others are a fall in prices (made possible by economies in technique, management, marketing or financing, or savings in raw material or labour costs); an improvement in quality; a change in design or packaging; and so on. Demand may also rise because of rising incomes, or a change in fashion or taste (itself often assisted by advertising). How far lower costs are passed on to the consumer in lower prices depends primarily on the degree of competition, actual or potential, from other

---

1   Editor's note: £2 15s in 1946 equates to £97 in 2014 prices! One shilling in 1958 equates to 99p in 2014 prices.

brands or commodities. Some or all of these factors were at work in the above examples and they have been at work ever since the Industrial Revolution in enlarging the scale of operations and reducing costs and prices. It is true that they have been disguised by inflation, especially since 1939, which has shrunk the value of the money unit; but apart from this, the general tendency is for technical progress to lower real costs.

How has advertising helped? It is seldom possible to be certain, but the circumstantial evidence would seem to support the general claim that it has accelerated these movements and reduced costs and prices faster than they otherwise would have fallen.

Alternative methods

Was advertising the best way of achieving this objective? Was it cheaper or faster than any other possible way: namely, a field force of commercial travellers, encouraging retailers by larger margins, appointing specialist wholesalers or selling agents, selling by post or calling round houses, even buying up wholesale and/or retail firms in order to speed up distribution? This is more difficult to judge. 'If I didn't advertise', Lord Mackintosh has said, 'I should have to treble my travellers. It would cost just as much and would be a lot more trouble. You may have an army of travellers, or a smaller number with advertising'.[2]

---

2   In an address to the Norwich and Norfolk Publicity Club, 1954.

But how far do advertisers really base their choice of marketing method on exact statistics and dependable knowledge? We may begin by supposing that manufacturers know what they are doing, and that, if they have chosen advertising rather than other marketing methods, it must be because they found it cheaper, or faster, or better in some other way. Margaret Hall, the Oxford economist, says: 'the seller advertises because he thinks that advertisement is the cheapest means of selling his goods [...] It seems likely that [...] he is not mistaken' (Hall 1949). Mr Taplin is more cautious: he says business men are not always right, although they try to be right because it pays them. This is the more valid claim. 'Advertising campaigns have failed to promote sales, and production and marketing costs have occasionally outrun sales [...] What is true [...] is that advertisers are as anxious as the public – in fact more anxious – not to waste their own resources and reputation in aimless, frivolous, or otherwise foolish advertising'.[3]

This is broadly true, although the level of company taxation blunts the incentive to keep costs to the lowest level possible. But the skill of the advertising agent, or advertising manager on the staff, will be used to press the claims of advertising while the claims of rival methods have not the ear of the managing director or equal access to the board room. It is possible, therefore, especially in the short run, that advertising is sometimes employed without investigation of the claims of alternative marketing methods.

---

3   *Journal of the Advertising Association*, February, 1958.

Moreover, there are even now no certain methods of tracing the effect on sales of an advertising campaign. When Lord Heyworth quoted his predecessor, Lord Leverhulme, as saying that half his advertising was wasted, but he never knew which half, the present chairman of Unilever contented himself with adding: 'We hope that we are on the way to bettering that score'.[4] Another great industrialist, Samuel Courtauld, went so far as to assert that 'most competitive advertising is a costly extravagance'. But in the long run, over industry as a whole, provided competition is active, rival firms will not lightly neglect ways of reducing costs, and it is likely that if advertising has been preferred to other marketing methods it is because it is believed to be better than other methods.

But in the meantime no more can be claimed than that manufacturers hope that advertising is the best available method of selling their goods. Advertising is far from being an exact science, although its practitioners have now many years of experience in employing the scientific method of trial and error. Great advances have been made, even since the end of the war. Consumer research based on accurate sampling can roughly identify the market to be won and suggest changes in the product, its packaging, presentation or price, designed to widen the welcome for it; ingenuity in copy-testing can produce effective selling appeals: statistical control of expenditure and scrupulous selection of media can minimise – but not avoid – abortive spending by eliminating irrelevant or duplicated circulation. But

4   In his annual address to Unilever shareholders, 1958.

the effect on sales of a given campaign cannot be isolated from the constantly changing forces at work in the market, and its efficiency cannot, therefore, be accurately assessed. It is less true than it was that, of all commercial expenditure, advertising is the most speculative. But advertising men are still like scientists seeking for the truth: they are getting nearer, but are still some way off.

We may, then, assume that advertising can increase output, but by how much? By the normal process of competition, cost reduction would have led manufacturers to reduce prices and this itself would have stimulated demand. The power of price-cuts to stimulate demand has often been under-estimated both by some economists and by businessmen. Demand is more responsive to price than is often supposed. The common notion that price is unimportant has been fostered by 20 years of inflation, but the advent of self-service stores and supermarkets has shown how questionable this notion is.

Stimulating demand

There are five ways in which advertising is claimed to increase the scale of production and reduce costs:

(a) by stimulating demand;
(b) by ironing out fluctuations in demand;
(c) by guiding demand into fewer channels;
(d) by displacing more costly methods of marketing;
(e) by sharpening competition.

Whatever the power of advertising to influence demand, the evidence compiled by the US economist Dr Neil Borden

(1942) suggests that it is exaggerated both by the critics and the users of advertising. New research may undermine the Borden findings, but, in the meantime, we must take them into account.

Dr Borden studied the effects of advertising on the demand for cigarettes, cigars and smoking tobacco, sugar, toothpaste, domestic sheeting, oranges, walnuts, lettuce, shoes, refrigerators, cars, petrol, breakfast foods, electric clocks, electric shavers, women's hosiery, wireless receivers, and many other commodities. His main conclusion was that:

> the basic trends of demand for products are determined primarily by underlying social and environmental conditions [...] advertising by itself serves not so much to increase demand for a product as to speed up the expansion of a demand that would come from favourable conditions, or to retard adverse trends due to unfavourable conditions.

Thus, he found that the demand for sugar, green vegetables and professional services had grown without much advertising. On the other hand, the demand for cigars, smoking tobacco, furniture, wheat flour, and men's shoes continued to fall despite heavy advertising.

This is what we should expect. No amount of advertising would have saved the canals from the railways, or the hansom cab from the taxi; and no advertising will now prevent the railways from losing ground to the long-distance lorry and the car.

It must also not be overlooked that many advertising campaigns are failures in the USA. It has been said that no less than 90 per cent of new products are abandoned because in some respect – price, quality, size, taste, colour, package, and so on – they do not 'catch on'. Here again the sovereignty of the consumer is far stronger than the critics – and even some supporters – of the free economy often suppose.

Where advertising did raise the demand for the product of an individual producer, Borden found it was for one or more of five reasons:

1. the most important was when the underlying psychological and physical conditions of the demand for the product as a whole were favourable: social standards, personal habits, fashion, incomes, the size and distribution of the population;

2. when it was possible to differentiate the product from its closest substitutes: thus advertising was more effective for cosmetics, refrigerators and cars than for sugar, salt or canned fruit;

3. when advertising could emphasise concealed properties (for example, in watches and washing machines); the features of fashion goods were external and could be judged by the consumer;

4. when appeal could be made to emotional buying motives – as in foods and drugs (health appeals) and cosmetics (vanity);

5. when sales were large enough to support the minimum advertising appropriations: cigarettes and toothpaste provided the sums out of larger turnover or high unit prices, but sugar and expensive clocks could not because their margins were too low or their turnover too small.

Reducing fluctuations

A second way in which advertising could reduce costs is by ironing out demand. There are many examples to show that it can even out seasonal fluctuations. The consumption of Wall's ice-cream has been raised in the winter months so that, in a few years, it has virtually changed from being a summer fad into an all-year-round food.

Over the longer fluctuations of booms and slumps, Kaldor has suggested that advertising may exacerbate the swing by stimulating demand in a boom, when there are high profits to spend on advertising, and slackening off in a slump, when profits fall. This is possible; but so also is the opposite. In the early 1930s when the commercial demand for shipping fell, advertising helped to create a new demand by popularising cruising. During the 1953–54 recession in the US, national income fell by 2.6 per cent from March 1953 to September 1954, but advertising expenditure was increased by 7 per cent. It is impossible to say how far spending and development was maintained by this means and the recession kept milder and shorter than it might have been. Advertising expenditure can be likened to Keynesian investment which generates incomes without adding to the output of consumer goods. Whatever the mechanics, it would appear that advertising need not necessarily decline when demand is flagging.

On the other hand, advertising tends to expand when demand is growing, especially if high taxation reduces its impact on profits; whether there is a case for stopping or reducing advertising in such circumstances is considered below.

Competition and choice

The third way in which advertising can reduce costs is by concentrating demand on fewer varieties. Black Magic, Macleans, Guinness and other examples we have studied support this claim, but price reductions may be needed to induce consumers to accept a smaller range of choice. Advertising may be used to direct demand into few channels; but it can also be used for the opposite purpose of emphasising differences in product varieties, and is supported by superficial but costly modifications in design, appearance or packaging in the effort to make each producer's variety distinguishable from others.

We have already considered the view that advertising is the most efficient or cheapest method of marketing and have reached the conclusion that, in the long run, and in competitive conditions this may be true, although it is not necessarily true in the short run and in all circumstances.

The fifth way in which advertising can reduce costs is by sharpening competition. In modern times, when mass advertising media are open to entrepreneurs at a modest cost in relation to the retail value of their output, there is less chance that really important inventions will fail to win a hearing with the consumer: all innovations stand a better chance of acceptance. The history of advertising, of the introduction of new products, and of the continual search for improvements, indicates that success in meeting consumer demands is itself a force attracting fresh competition. There are unceasing efforts to imitate all successful products, or go one better, in order to climb on the bandwagon.

The pioneer who invests heavily in research and advertising to establish a new market is often making it easier for challengers to follow in his wake with much less expense. Consumers may generally welcome the new product but they like a choice, and few brands can for long be all things to all people. The case studies of Formica, Hoover washing machines, Toni perms, Lucozade, Polycell, and some of the other products we were able to examine lend supporting evidence for this thesis. Their manufacturers, in supplying us detailed information, displayed confidence that they could meet competition as it emerged and as the markets grew in size. Three recently launched products, from widely different fields, which appear classic examples of the pioneer whose advertising success is provoking keen competition from rivals new and old, are Rael Brook shirts, Babycham perry and G-Plan furniture.[5] Unfortunately there is no evidence available to allow us to judge the part advertising played in their initial success.

In a dynamic economy, the long-run benefit of advertising is that it can be used to enable a new product to enter a field dominated by established brands. Although advertising can be used defensively (and expensively) to protect established brands, and to launch 'indistinguishable' new brands, its justification is that, in the long run, it sharpens competition among manufacturers in providing the consumer with greater choice in style, price, quality, service, convenience and other product attributes.

---

5   Editor's note: All three brands are still in existence.

Too much innovation?

We must now consider the view that advertising is not necessarily beneficial if it accelerates changes that would have come about without it. If it quickens the growth in the scale of production, or the rate at which new commodities or services are introduced, the resources so used are not available for the production of other things. The benefit of the increased output of the first must be balanced against the loss of the second. There is nothing in economics that enables us to say that the gain always outweighs the loss. That people buy advertised goods is not by itself evidence that they prefer them to unadvertised goods: they may have no choice.

Nevertheless, this objection must be considered part of the wider problem of judging the beneficence of advertising that we have considered earlier. If advertising leads consumers to buy things they would not buy if left to their own devices, then it may be wasteful and anti-social. And there are obviously cases in which this can happen. But in the long run consumers acquire experience, by testing the offerings of advertisers and discussing among themselves, or with experts, the claims made for different products. Talk of 'captive audiences' is certainly exaggerated: because consumers can assert themselves against any amount of advertising, accepting or rejecting the commodities to which it has drawn their attention, the power of advertising to distort the pattern of spending is limited. This is the position we have taken up, because the argument and the evidence are on balance in its favour. The possibility that progress and innovation may be too fast and in the wrong directions cannot be ignored, but it does not radically alter the case for advertising we have already argued. In any event, the issue cannot be decided by reference to narrow, national requirements: least of all for Britain, which depends for survival upon exporting a quarter of its output, in the form dictated by foreign consumers and in competition with aggressive trade rivals that exploit every device to promote their sales.

A guarantee of quality and value?

So much for the claim of advertising to increase output and reduce costs by stimulating or regulating demand. Is it, however, a guarantee of quality or value for the consumer?

We have argued that for, many commodities, the consumer does not want detailed information on composition and performance, and that he is content to rely on the advice of retailers or friends, or on the brand-name attached by the manufacturer. Can the brand be represented as evidence, freely accepted by the consumer, that the commodity will be (a) of a known quality and standard, and (b) the best value available on the market?

There seems little doubt that the first of these claims is valid. 'There is [...] real spiritual comfort', says Professor Sir Dennis Robertson (1958), 'in buying a packet of a known and trusted brand of cocoa rather than a shovelful of brown powder of uncertain origin.' A brand-name is a convenient shorthand that saves the wholesaler, retailer and purchaser time and argument. It thus simplifies distribution, and to this extent reduces costs. In every shop, in every part of the country, even in every part of the world, a known brand-name indicates a commodity of dependable qualities and performance. If the quality is not maintained, the maker is exposed to be shot at. 'When you advertise you are like a man going bail for his behaviour on his own recognisances for a very substantial sum', Sir Miles Thomas has justifiably told advertisers.[6] Even Phineas Barnum knew the customer's power: 'You may advertise a spurious article and induce many people to call and buy it once, but they will gradually denounce you as an imposter'. The truth is that consumers do not meekly accept the guarantee of quality or standard unquestioningly: the housewife has been quick to listen to suspicions about the apparently smaller amount of detergents in packets sold with coupon price reductions.

The guarantee of value is more complex. Ostensibly there would appear to be blatant examples to the contrary. Patent medicines are often quoted: some can be obtained unbranded at a fraction of the retail price asked for the branded package.[7] Some goods are sold at varying prices under different names, or at a lower price without a name. But what are consumers buying? They are buying not merely commodities with physical properties but subjective satisfactions which cannot be measured by the

---

6   Address to the Sheffield Publicity Club, 1955.

7   The first issue of *Which?* suggested that there was no significant difference between aspirin tablets selling at 4d for 25 and the branded varieties costing between three and five times as much.

onlooker. It is this which imposes limitations on the usefulness of consumer advisory services that must necessarily be concerned only with objective characteristics. If a brand-name brings additional pleasure, who shall say the consumer is foolish to pay a higher price?

There is here a philosophical principle concerning choice and personal responsibility which we discuss in the next chapter. In the meantime, it is pertinent to argue that competitive advertising stimulates product improvement. There is a constant search for some new feature (or 'plus point') which might keep a brand ahead of its rivals and about which the manufacturer can boast in his advertisements. Useful examples are found in detergents, furniture, washing machines, toys, electric shavers (even razor blades), margarines, garden tools and many other fields.

Advertising as an incentive

The third claim made for advertising is that, by sharpening incentives to acquire the commodities or services advertised, it stimulates effort and output and raises living standards. As with the effect of advertising on technical improvement and production, the claim can be formulated more modestly and more conveniently by introducing the time element: by stimulating the wish to acquire goods and services, advertising raises living standards sooner or faster than they otherwise would rise. Although factual evidence cannot easily be assembled, the claim in this form would appear incontrovertible.

Illustrations can be quoted in plenty. The large increase in the ownership of labour-saving or pleasure-giving household appliances since the end of the war has undoubtedly been expedited by advertising, and has itself increased national output by keeping men working overtime and inducing married women to go out to work.

In general terms, the point has rarely been better put than by Sir Winston Churchill:[8]

> Advertising nourishes the consuming power of men. It creates wants for a better standard of living. It sets up before a man the goal of a better home, better clothing, better food for himself and for his family. It spurs individual exertion and greater production.

The statesman is joined by a moralist: the Rev Dr W. E. Sangster courageously approved of material aspirations:

> The luxuries of one generation become the necessities of the next [...] Those of us who are over 50 years of age know the slavery of the housewife. Then science came to her aid and took a large part of the drudgery out of housework. Demand fostered by advertising made it possible to produce labour-saving devices at prices which enable nearly everybody to buy them.[9]

And a trade union leader, Sir Tom Williamson, makes a formidable trio:[10]

---

8   At the Wembley Exhibition, 1924.

9   Advertising Association Conference, 1953.

10 Advertising Association Conference, 1955.

Never before has advertising better demonstrated to us all how many things there are to have to make life easier, more comfortable and more enjoyable. Most of these aids to good living are intended, not for the few only, but for an expanding range of people. But we must work for them.

Worlds to conquer

For some years during the post-war inflation, the incentive effect of advertising was overlooked by the superficial political and moral critic of advertising, who saw it merely as an unhealthy stimulant to spending in a period of inflation and who called for the repression of advertising by taxation, or for the suppression of television financed by advertising. It was left to economists to put the issue into perspective. Mrs Honor Croome put the politicians and the moralists in their place in a few paragraphs:[11]

> The appeal to spend is not merely an appeal to rush out, withdraw savings, and buy this or that product. It is an appeal to raise one's standard of living, set one's sights higher all round [...] the report of the Anglo-American Productivity Team stressed the contrast between the American working man, whose motto as regards his standard is 'the sky's the limit', and his British counterpart, who, by and large, loses all interest in extra production and earnings as soon as his existing standard is safely provided for. [...] In the right economic setting, a rousing television campaign for better living, whetting appetites, awakening ambition, could be just what this country needs.

11 *Western Mail*, 24 September 1955.

It is now a far cry since John Burns' lament that 'the tragedy of the working man is the poverty of his desires'. Mrs Croome reminds us that the British wage-earner does not aim nearly so high as the American; but his horizon is far wider than it was: he now aspires to middle-class standards. And we should rejoice. Yet moralists and aesthetes question his striving for better material conditions of life. These arrogant autocrats, who normally enjoy high standards of comfort themselves, indulge in lofty laments about cultural and spiritual progress lagging behind the material. They decry ambition and striving to improve one's lot in life as though it were unworthy. Yet, as Samuel Johnson said, making money (and, therefore, getting what money can buy: spiritual as well as material satisfaction) is one of the more innocent ways in which man can be employed. The world would be more peaceful if people were allowed to trade freely together than if they are aroused by mystics moved by so-called cultural values.

In any event, man is still deplorably poor. Yet a reputable economist has seriously argued that the age of affluence has arrived. Professor J. K. Galbraith (1958) affects to see in the useless elongations and gaudy decorations of motor cars evidence that living standards (in the US) are now so high that scarcity has been, or is being, abolished. Far from this being a new economic theory, it is old hat. It harks back to that musty myth of the inter-war years which proclaimed that the problem of production had been solved and that all that remained was to distribute the superabundance. It harks back even further to the Marxist mirage of Lenin, who once dreamed of building communism on a new race of selfless men and on the abolition of money and scarcity. The truth is that scarcity will remain with man as long as his aspirations outpace his achievements. 'Scarcity' does not mean absolute want, but want relative to existing resources. In this sense, 'scarcity' is a necessary accompaniment of a progressive society. It could be abolished tomorrow if the peoples of the world suddenly became satisfied with their lot. If scarcity vanished, so also would ambition and striving for improvement.

The 'abolition of scarcity' could only mean the replacement of progressiveness, even at modest living standards, by stagnation and decadence, even at high living standards. What gives life zest and purpose is the drive for better things tomorrow. Robert Browning put the point with beauty: 'Ah, but a man's reach should exceed his grasp. Or what's a heaven for?'

We are here back with Marshall, Knight and Coase: a full life is not acceptance of what we have, but the urge to improve it. That is man at his best – from the one who tinkers to find a way to mend his child's toy, to the one who climbs Everest. There is no scarcity of worlds to conquer.

In Britain today, the average man and woman still spend far too much of their lives labouring. For five days in seven, men spend most of their daylight hours at work, and mostly at tasks that give little pleasure or satisfaction. The typical American has a standard of living two or three times as high; yet he is poor even in material terms: one in three American town dwellers do not own a car, and one in two lives in someone else's house. A doubling in British living standards in 25 years would still leave the average

British family worse off than the average American family is now. It would certainly not exhaust the possibilities of improvement.

Conceptions of living standards are normally much too static. What is a common accompaniment of everyday life today was a luxury yesterday and non-existent the day before; and what today is beyond the reach of most people could tomorrow become a common base for still higher aspirations. If advertising can help to accelerate the pace at which luxuries become necessaries, it should hold a high place as an instrument of progress.

4   SOVEREIGN OR PUPPET?

We have argued that advertising has become an essential instrument for the wide distribution of mass-produced goods and for building up new markets. Properly used, it penetrates barriers of ignorance or indifference, challenges established producers or traders, and cuts a path for innovators to reach the consumer. But it remains no more than an instrument: like a pen, it serves the purposes of each hand that chooses to take it up. It can be handled skillfully as a rapier, clumsily as a bludgeon, deceitfully as a dagger, or lightly almost as a feather.

Advertising per se is neither uneconomic nor unethical (to take the two chief criticisms), although it can be and sometimes is used wastefully or insincerely. If competition is effective, the price of waste will be paid by the advertiser; but whenever advertising succeeds in misleading consumers it damages the public interest. Not even the most uncompromising critic proposes that advertising should be prohibited, any more than the most hostile pedestrian would seriously demand an end to motoring and public transport on grounds of safety or amenity. For motoring, reformers urge safer cars and roads, more parking facilities, better driving tuition and road courtesy, supported by more severe penalties for law-breakers; by such means road accidents may be reduced, but they will never be eliminated.

The way of reform in advertising is even more difficult: training and self-discipline have curbed excesses over much of the field, but anyone may write an advertisement, and no newspaper proprietor can ensure that everything advertised in his columns is described accurately. Advertisers do not need to be licensed like motorists, but their activities are under constant public surveillance, and are subject to laws designed to prevent fraud and misrepresentation and to protect public health and safety.

The scope for bad advertising should not be exaggerated. Because advertisements are used to sell almost every conceivable product and service, they offer a large target for those whose real objection is to the thing advertised. People who disapprove of betting, smoking, drinking, hire purchase, self-medication, birth control, Roman Catholicism or 'Billy Graham' campaigns, all find advertisements to condemn; and they are joined by those who object to the intrusion of commerce into their comfortable lives. No doubt advertising mirrors the imperfections of human society, but we shall not waste much time on critics who aim at the reflected image instead of declaring openly against smoking or gambling or hire purchase or whatever it is they dislike. While the law permits such activities, their advertising must be tolerated.

Yet in the final analysis, advertising cannot be justified simply because it helps producers sell their wares. In our discussion we follow the teaching of Adam Smith that 'the interest of the producer ought to be attended to only so far as is necessary for promoting that of the consumer'. It is precisely because it tends to impel producers to serve the consumer that the system of open markets must form the basis of a free society.

Sovereignty in theory

The general argument for allowing consumers the widest possible choice in spending their money is that no one knows the individual's wants better than he does himself, and, since none is able to satisfy every want, each will get the best value from his limited income by spending and saving as he thinks best. Those who suspect that this approach makes too much of the diversity of human wants might reflect that no two people (from choice) dress the same, no two larders are similarly stocked, no two libraries comprise identical books. Many differences may be ascribed to personal fads, foibles or prejudices, but these are exactly what the individual knows as his personal preferences. Some spending is certainly the outcome of chance or ignorance, but the case for consumer sovereignty does not rest on the assumption that choices are made in the light of full knowledge of alternatives. Since a pound spent in one way is at the expense of a pound spent in every other possible way, a perfectly informed choice is seldom made. That is inevitable – the more so as higher living standards multiply the choices open to us. It is no reason for imagining that, by any method of centralising decisions about consumption, the planners could match the dynamic diversity of personal preferences more closely than the free market, imperfect as it may be.

We are here at the heart of the philosophical nature of demand and human satisfaction. If an inferior product is bought or a higher price paid by the consumer in ignorance, the remedy appears plain: supply more information. But what if the information is available and not needed? The authoritarian might say: 'Compel the public to act on it'. But a better answer for our kind of society would be: 'Try to persuade them, but if they still prefer their vanities let them pay the price – so long as their health and safety are not endangered'. As Sir Arnold Plant has said, economists should welcome greater rationality of choice in the sense that 'the fewest possible subsequent regrets occur due to mistakes'. Living in a free society is one way of learning to make the best use of all it offers: freedom includes the liberty to choose badly as a means of learning to choose well.

When John Stuart Mill argued that it was more important that choice should be free than that it should be good, he acknowledged that liberty was a principle suited only to adult societies: it could not safely be applied until 'mankind have become capable of being improved by free and equal discussion'. 'Until then', he regretted, 'there is nothing for them but implicit obedience to an Akbar or a Charlemagne if they are so fortunate as to find one'.

Three generations of elementary education and two of secondary education have provided the most fundamental defence against appeals to ignorance and the emotions. Despite the mutterings of muddled middle-roaders, critics who boggle at occasional excesses should understand that the broad choice remains between giving consumers their heads or handing over to a lesser breed of Akbars and Charlemagnes. If education has not yet taught everyone how to choose wisely, there is no other way for a free society than to try to expedite its processes. We may think that some choices are deplorable, but we must not go on to argue that there should be no choices. The dilemma is illustrated by Richard Hoggart in his study of working-class culture, *The Uses of Literacy*. He argues that, despite greater educational opportunities, newspapers and magazines are marked by 'an increased trivialisation'. Although he sees the difficulty of official interference in a democracy, he thinks that its cultural developments may be 'as dangerous in their own way as those we are shocked at in totalitarian societies'. Nevertheless, he ends on a hopeful note:

> working-class people, though they are being in a sense exploited today, at least have now to be approached for their consent. The force of environment and the powers of persuasion count for a great deal but they are not irresistible.

It is a natural anxiety among those who are sensitive to the abuses of freedom to want to make people choose rightly; the unavoidable risks of freedom and its power as an educator are not always seen as clearly. By and large the public knows what it wants, and it is not necessarily true that the least literate are the most easily fooled, although being less articulate they may find it difficult to give clear reasons for their choices. One consideration above all should trouble those concerned with culture and education: it is easy for them to decry the choices made by a group or a class, but in decrying specific choices they are also decrying the system that makes free choice possible. If people are not competent to choose their magazines, are they competent to choose their Members of Parliament? And, if they are not, who is competent to choose better? Nothing much has really been added to this discussion since Mill wrote *On Liberty*.

Sovereignty in practice: consumer and citizen

This last point needs emphasis. In a Fabian pamphlet, *Efficiency and the Consumer*, the author, C. D. Harbury, dismisses consumers' sovereignty as 'no more than an empty slogan', and compares the dilemma of 'the average consumer [...] in a large number of important purchases every day' to that of a 'young Indian from the swamps of the Amazon' let loose in the British Museum to make a 'sensible selection' of books. After scorning the way choice is influenced by 'irrational motives' (custom, national, religious and other traditions), and by advertisers appealing to fashion and emulation (scented stockings, 'Elvis Presley' cosmetics, etc.), Mr. Harbury decides that the analogy with an Amazonian native is an over-simplification: 'It might have been more appropriate', he says:

> to present him standing in the library with all the members of the staff shouting at him that the books they have are the best [...] while he is searching for books with the prettiest colours, best pictures, or even the most attractive smells.

Thus the professed saviours of the consumer, in the Webbian tradition, display their contempt for the common sense, intelligence and discrimination of men and women. When the Commons debated the need for a Royal Commission on advertising, many of the speeches revealed the same arrogant contempt for the consumer's ability to see through the exaggeration, insincerity and stupidity of advertisements. During an earlier debate, Mr Anthony Greenwood lamented that people were deceived by detergent advertising 'just as at election times, unfortunately, they are deceived by the propaganda from the [Conservative] party opposite'.

Mr Greenwood's complaint is significant because, in addition to showing that what 'deceives' depends on personal judgement, it draws attention to the essential similarity between commercial advertising and political propaganda. Politicians must stop giving themselves airs. If a voter is to be invited to read rival election addresses, he must be trusted to choose between rival advertisements. It does not matter that, as Mr Harbury says, most advertising is 'largely persuasive in character and the information supplied is selective'. The same applies to the election addresses. In the Commons' debate on a Royal Commission for advertising, a Labour MP, Mr Frederick Willey, pointed out that all propaganda requires 'balance', and went on to admit: 'Every hon. Member would be disturbed if he felt there was not to be a reply to what he said'. So would most commercial advertisers. Even if the point was bluntly made by Mr Willey, he expressed the difference between the approach of the democrat and that of the authoritarian.

A Conservative MP who was also a director of an advertising agency, Mr Graham Page, suggested that many shortcomings of advertising would be remedied if the government discharged its own advertising responsibilities more effectively. He described road safety advertising as 'disgraceful [...] no sort of campaign to meet one of the greatest tragedies of our time', and urged better government advertising to prevent accidents in homes and factories, promote preventive medicine and publicise opportunities in advanced education.

In a democracy the individual is exposed to many sources of information and persuasion. He may complain of a surfeit of advice; he may decide to close his ears and appeal to his friends or to independent experts; he may learn by trial and error what to accept and what to reject: but he is better off than the victims of a state monopoly in persuasion. Experience in every totalitarian country shows that, even after years of indoctrination aimed at ironing out individual preferences, compulsion remains the chief instrument of government. In practice the choice is not between verbal persuasion and physical coercion. A free society relies on a great deal of the first and a minimum of the second; but a state-controlled community gets more of both, with the difference that the 'persuasion', being censored, is itself mental coercion.

Those who declaim against persuasion are running away from the problem. There can be no escape from it in the modern world. The question is whether it shall be private (and visible) persuasion, with some hope of mitigating its excesses, wastes and abuses, or state persuasion, with the ever-present risk that it will degenerate into veiled coercion. The individual's best defence lies in a variety of persuaders, and that is what a competitive society operating within a framework of liberal institutions provides.

Satisfaction for consumers

No amount of information or advice will prevent consumers buying things that appear more expensive or of lower quality than equally accessible alternatives. This is sometimes due to carelessness or stupidity, or to a calculated indifference about saving money, especially if it would mean spending time shopping around. But frequently a purchase that strikes the onlooker as 'irrational' is the result of a different opinion about the 'best buy' in the circumstances of the individual purchaser. Alternative brands are seldom perfect substitutes, and even when one can be objectively proved superior on every count, it is unlikely to appear as desirable in the eye of all beholders.

A comparison between rival brands based upon the test of utility is often beside the point and invariably misleading, because it over-simplifies the issue. When economists talk of 'utility' as the foundation of values, they mean not 'usefulness' but something much wider, namely 'satisfaction'. In a primitive community there may be a high correlation between these two concepts: things are satisfying in proportion to their usefulness in overcoming hunger, danger and cold. But prosperous societies are no longer concerned with fuelling basic needs for food, protection, clothing and accommodation in their crude forms. As Professor

Frank Knight wrote in *Ethics of Competition* (1935), we 'become so "particular" as to their mode of gratification that the form dominates the substance'. Each want becomes refined into a constellation of different wants, and in seeking to satisfy them new or associated wants are developed. Demand ceases to reflect simple physical needs; it will become as varied as the permutations of temperament, taste, training, intelligence and individual personality.

In his classic Cambridge handbook, *Demand and Supply*, the late Sir Hubert Henderson wrote: 'We greatly deceive ourselves if we suppose wealth to be an objective reality', and as an illustration he gave the following example:

> A pair of boots is an objective fact; so is the number of pairs in existence, so is their size, their weight, the quantity of leather or paper which they happen to contain. But the wealth which those boots represent is not an objective fact. It depends upon the opinion which men and women entertain as to their utility; and these opinions take us into the subjective regions of human psychology.

Professor Lionel Robbins has put it: 'nothing is valuable but thinking makes it so'. A free society must rest upon the decisions that men and women make for themselves as consumers. Because wants are so varied, there is plenty of room for manufacturers to compete in supplying substitute satisfactions. No consumer will be able to match his exact requirements because he cannot afford to have his furniture, house, car, garden, and so on, tailor-made to individual specifications; but the greater variety of choice – even between almost identical alternatives – the more closely he can satisfy his particular wants.

Because wants are subjective there is wide scope for advertisers to invest products with different shades of satisfactions to match the opinions of different consumers. In such cases the advertisement becomes part and parcel of the product it advertises. This has led an American writer to suggest that a theory of advertising can be built on the premise that it 'adds a new value to the product' (Abbott 1956). A leading British practitioner, Mr John Hobson, has expressed the view that since 'consumers are seeking experiences not things', advertising (and indeed all sources of information):

> [adds] subjective qualities to a product, for example in giving a feeling of smartness, cheerfulness, rightness, wellbeing, etc., in the choice or use of the product, and thus increasing its ability to satisfy a yet more ramified, but just as real, complex of wants.

What critics regard as 'wasteful product differentiation' is a continuous process by which manufacturers attempt to match the opinions of different groups of consumers about what a product should be like. Sometimes it takes the form of investing a brand with distinction, such as with Parker pens, Ronson lighters and Rolls Royce cars; with other products it is the romantic, glamorous, traditional, or even avant garde associations that are evoked by presentation, packaging and advertising. The performance and quality of the product remain important but its 'personality' or 'brand image' contributes to the satisfaction of ownership.

Those who complain about the uniformity of modern societies brought about by improved education and communications miss the fact that changing conditions have also enormously increased the variety of housing, furniture, dress, entertainments, hobbies and even of intellectual pursuits. Professor Knight might almost have been writing an advertisement for advertising when he said: 'The development of wants is really much more important than their satisfaction; there is no poverty so deplorable as the poverty of ideas'.

In the Fabian pamphlet referred to earlier, Mr Harbury concludes with an impassioned appeal for more education so that consumers become 'capable of objective decision-making and deliberate action'. No doubt schools, universities, women's associations, broadcasting authorities and other instruments of instruction have a part to play in promoting greater discrimination, not only about buying and selling, but also about living, marrying, bringing up children and occupying the leisure which a prosperous economy confers in growing measure. But Mr Harbury's aim of imposing upon the public a 'science of consumption' lacks realism as well as human understanding. Advertisers and their agents cannot be blamed for the imperfections of human nature. Moralists may censure them for taking advantage of human weakness, and for exploiting the worst rather than appealing to the best in us. But the human spirit is not lightly trifled with: advertisers who aim low often find that they have missed the target. Some have failed to interpret the social changes of our day and allow for advances in tastes and standards. We can get some idea of the trend of consumer discrimination by looking at what is happening in America. Professor Paul Samuelson writes:

there are some signs that the American consumer is becoming pretty professional these days. Item: prodigious growth of cut-price supermarkets that sell us groceries at an extremely low markup. Item: marked growth of 'discount houses' that sell durable appliances far below 'list prices'. Item: mushrooming of the 'do-it-yourself' movement, whereby we quit work on Saturdays and paint our own rooms. Only observe a young couple about to buy a high-fidelity phonograph set. Note their hours of careful study and field work. What Arabian master of the art of buying and selling can match their professional competence? What laboratory scientists, their meticulous zeal?

Yet some who aim low are getting good results, at least in the short run. The solution lies partially in the restraint and the foresight that is reflected in voluntary codes. But more generally the elevation of tastes and human conduct is a national problem that calls for patient education, example and leadership at every level. There is always room for improvement; in the meantime people will get the advertising they want, just as politically they get the government they want. No amount of advertising will continue to sell products that do not satisfy consumers – certainly not dishonest advertising. That is no reason for tolerating advertisements that are false and misleading, because they waste resources while consumers are experimenting and learning what satisfies them best.

Let the advertiser beware

When Mr Noel-Baker called for a Royal Commission on advertising he was careful to preface his attack on 'dishonest practices, swindles and rackets' by declaring that advertising 'is an integral part of business life [...] (and) is perfectly legitimate and reputable'. It is to this form of criticism that advertising is most vulnerable, and there is growing evidence of hostility towards some of its excesses. In August 1958, Gallup Poll conducted a survey of public opinion about advertising. It revealed that, while 74 per cent of those asked acknowledged the importance of advertising in Britain, and 84 per cent agreed it rendered a useful service in telling about new products, only 30 per cent thought it kept down prices, and the majority of those who expressed an opinion thought too much was spent on advertising. More support came from the 25–34 year olds than from younger or older groups, from Conservatives and Liberals than from Socialists, and from men than from women. Of the 72 per cent who expressed a view on whether advertising should be taxed, almost one half declared in favour. Comparison with surveys in January and June 1958 shows a decline in public favour for the industry. One of the Gallup Poll conclusions was: 'Perhaps advertising has done a better job in selling other people than it has done in selling itself'.

In the US similar trends are in evidence. The 1958 conference of the American Association of Advertising Agents was told of an intensive series of interviews conducted by the Institute of Public Opinion among one hundred American women. This revealed general approval and interest mixed with resentment against false and base appeals in advertisements. One in two women associated advertising with 'exaggeration', one in four or five with 'misleading' and 'poor taste', and one in twenty with 'dishonesty'. In answer to specific questions, 86 agreed that 'some advertising is dishonest' and 71 that some is 'an insult to people's intelligence'.

The growth in public criticism of advertising cannot be due to any general lowering of standards, because in both countries higher codes of practice are supported by legal sanctions that did not exist thirty years ago. A possible explanation is the post-war increase in advertising and particularly in commercial television which is more obtrusive than press and posters. But the most important reason for keener public criticism is the increase in education, experience, knowledge and sophistication among modern consumers.

Advertisers and their critics must see how this affects the argument. The fact that people are on their guard against exaggeration and deception means that the power of advertising to do damage is weakened. It also means that misleading advertising is wasteful and in the long run doomed to failure. Advertisers, agencies and media owners should learn from the disgust that people feel about the appeals exploited in some advertisements. There may always be honest differences of opinion about how far the enthusiastic salesman can go without overstepping the limits of permissible exaggeration; but the time may be approaching, if it has not arrived, when the moderate, reasoned appeal will have a better chance of achieving the desired results. That is the opinion of the most experienced and successful advertising practitioners of today. Mr Cecil Notley told the 1955 conference of the Advertising Association:

It is extraordinary how insincere and trivial a lot of 'forceful' copy sounds when it is read out aloud. I recommend the exercise to you. Would it not be better to be a little more reasonable, to restrain our language a trifle and treat our readers like intelligent human beings rather than as deaf dolts who must be shouted at?

Mr David Ogilvy, who is generally acclaimed and envied as one of the outstandingly successful exponents of British advertising in the US, has said: 'My whole thesis is that you can write a hard-selling ad without clichés and dullness. The trouble with most copy is that it is written below the average intelligence. I would rather write a little above it.'

The success of practitioners of what has been called 'an almost blatant appeal to good taste' must encourage others to raise their sights. Those who persist in shouting their trivial and tedious advertisements are functioning, in the words of Dr Michael Young (the founder-chairman of Consumers' Association), as 'chief recruiting agents' for consumer advisory organisations.

The role of the consumer

Purged of its excesses, advertising takes its place as one among many influences that help shape the pattern of consumption. It is well-known that good advertising may not succeed in selling a bad product, just as a good product may sell despite ineffective advertising. Examples of failures are for obvious reasons difficult to document, but we have privately studied several cases of brands of cigarettes, medicines and toilet goods which flopped after a great deal of expense and ingenuity had been devoted to their advertising. We have also studied confidential reports that show how relatively unimportant advertising may be, compared with recommendations from friends, relatives, retailers, doctors and so on. In the case of brands currently advertised on television, it is not uncommon for 30 per cent of those questioned to attribute their first purchase to the advertising, but they are outnumbered by those who buy on personal recommendation. In other cases, advertising directly accounts for a much smaller proportion of purchases, although it may have had an unconscious influence on the 20 or 25 per cent who cannot recall what caused them to try the brand.

Perhaps the advertisements most frequently considered as objectionable are those for detergents. It is not so much that people (television viewers particularly) object to the 'white lies', as that they grow hostile to the tedious repetition of the strident claims night after night. When members of the Consumers' Association were asked to name products that they would like to have tested, 25 per cent of the 10,000 who replied named detergents; paints, refrigerators, carpets, toothpaste and petrol came a long way behind. Undoubtedly the reason is that the public does not believe that there is as much to choose between them as the rival advertisements loudly insist.

Three comments might be offered. In the first place, the consumers are not unaware of the rival claims, and that is itself some protection against being 'taken in' by any one advertiser.

Secondly, even if there is not much to choose between the different brands today, there was five years ago – and there may be again a year or two hence. The fact that competitive products for the mass market are often very similar in quality and performance is a tribute to the way in which research and imitation rob the brand leader of its initial superiority.

The third comment is that, however tedious detergent and other hard-selling advertising may be, the degree to which it can inflate costs is limited. Boots, Marks & Spencer, Sainsbury's and other chain retailers can challenge manufacturers' branded goods by offering their own unadvertised products at a marked price advantage. Boots now sells its own brand of anti-freeze for car radiators, Sainsbury's sells many grocery lines made to its own specifications, and Marks & Spencer has extended its 'St Michael' brand from clothing to foodstuffs. If the popular detergents (or any other heavily advertised goods) reach the point where price becomes over-loaded with advertising costs, such retailers will be presented with an opportunity to encroach on their markets, using the power of a significant price reduction.

The fact remains that, while superficial copy-writers are trying to think up better advertisements, the soap manufacturers are searching for still better products to advertise. If we value choice, irritating advertisements may have to be suffered, at least until one of the leading advertisers heeds the advice of David Ogilvy and breaks away from the tiresome repetition of largely meaningless appeals. Meanwhile, there are many other fields in which advertising is performing a valuable service in spreading news about interesting developments that are gradually changing the pattern of living.

However imperfectly the present system may appear to work, it remains preferable to any practicable alternative. The strident clash of rival claims is better than the silent indifference of monopolists. So long as consumers have choice, they are in less need of protection than the victims of monopoly, not least when operated by the state. It is only since the Independent Television Authority (ITA) was established in 1955 that the BBC has avoided being a target for the kind of impotent criticism now directed at the National Coal Board and British Railways. Until the critics of private enterprise and private advertising can show what alternatives would serve the community better, a little modesty in their claims would become them.

Most of the failings of advertising are capable of remedy, within the limits of imperfect human society. Few customers are misled, or if they are misled once they learn to watch out the next time. And for expensive items of domestic equipment, such as television sets, washing machines and refrigerators, they are not usually so impulsive that they will act on the testimony of any one manufacturer's advertisements: as we have seen, there are a great many other sources of information and advice open to them. In short, consumers acquire more sales resistance than sensitive reformers suppose. Certainly no experienced advertiser regards customers as tame puppets who will dance to his tune – any more than the politician can so regard the electorate, particularly as an election approaches. Indeed, the businessman treats the consumer with something like awe and respect compared with the treatment meted out to the voter by the politician who employs half-truths, quarter-truths, exaggerations, distortions and terminological inexactitudes.

Let the buyer beware

It is fashionable to regard the common law doctrine of caveat emptor ('let the buyer beware') as having been outmoded by a great deal of statute law which for many decades has weighted the scales in the consumer's favour. We must recall that it is not the duty of the government in a free society to relieve individuals of the responsibility for spending (or saving) their money and accepting the consequences. There is always room for argument about where the lines should be drawn between public and private initiative, but it must be clear that the continuous extension of government control threatens to rob personal responsibility of substance and significance. Well-meaning attempts to remedy defects in our economic institutions have often aggravated the original trouble and provided excuses for still more restrictions that usually burdened consumers with higher prices or restricted their choice. The history of tariffs, rent restriction, betting and licensing provide examples of policies that proved easier to adopt when there seemed good reason for them than to abolish when they had outlived their day. On the contrary, a society shows itself to be free to the degree that it widens the range of choices, despite the risks.

There is still much that is irritating, vulgar, or otherwise objectionable about advertising, but so long as people value the freedom to buy what pleases them, they should not be too quick to complain about advertising and sales-manship: the coin that has the sovereign consumer on one side carries the image of the salesman on the other. Sales-manship, both commercial and political, is universally practised in free societies and distinguishes them from tyrannies where personal choice, again both commercial and political, is confined to taking or leaving what suits those in control.

No doubt the salesman (or politician) will press his wares in season and out of season, and if he does not great-ly exaggerate their merits, he must be expected at least to talk well of them. Every reputable manufacturer who pits his product against competition believes it of better value or more closely suited to the needs of some consumers. The case for honesty in trade was well expressed by Sir Miles Thomas in a broadcast when he said that 'only a bad sales-man would wish, by deliberate misrepresentation of the product he is selling, to talk himself out of his profession for the sake of possible short-term gains'. We may doubt whether short-sighted salesmen are as rare as Sir Miles im-plied, although misrepresentation is easier in conversation on the housewife's doorstep than in prominently displayed advertisements.

Sir Miles, however, pitched his defence of salesman-ship higher than the level of commercial necessity: 'All nature', he argued, 'is imbued with the instinct of selling', and from the example of the peacock he held that every employer, employee, politician, author, educationalist, preacher and philosopher was in some sense trying to sell something to others. In a comment on the broadcast, *The*

Listener accepted this wider interpretation of salesmanship but, with typical obstinacy, regretted that there was too much of it. Then, after quoting another talk in which Angus Maude warned against 'exaggeration, euphemism, and even a measure of mild deception in advertising and [political] propaganda', it concluded:

> As Thomas Hobbes said many years ago, words are counters which can be used to win a game. And words will always need to be closely analysed and scrutinised by those who do not wish to be overwhelmed by high-powered salesmanship.

The case for caveat emptor could not be put more plainly. The citizen of a free society must keep his wits about him and make his own decisions. All the help that can be devised for him – the trademarks, kitemarks, informative labels, consumer advice, education and warning – are road signs and signposts to guide him on his way, not to tell him what his destination should be. In the last resort he must be the master of his fate. He must weigh what he is told by advertisers, traders, politicians and neighbours, and discard what he finds wanting, particularly when any of them are seeking his custom or support. That is the privilege, and the price, of freedom.

APPENDIX A: THE DETERGENT HALO

Many of the common criticisms of advertising – that it is wasteful, wearisome, bogus and brash – seem to be exhibited in the advertising of detergents.

'The whole object of advertising is to build a halo round the article', said William Lever in 1909 of his plans for selling soap. It would seem to be even truer of detergents. There appears to be something unreal about the reputations built up for detergents, and the large claims, the pseudo-scientific evidence, and the extravagant language add to the impression of a gigantic game in which firms build up sales by hoodwinking and bamboozling the bewildered housewife.

Whatever the chemical composition of the detergents and their relative efficiency as materials for doing the humdrum job of washing clothes and dishes, the whole business of selling them has been built up on a jungle of jingles, slogans and catch-phrases that may be effective in introducing the commodities to the customer and reminding her of them but which lend themselves to parody and satire. The result is that, because the copywriters have been given their heads, the solid virtues of the detergents and the methods by which they are being marketed have been fogged by a mist of make-believe. And, because the leading manufactures are engaged in such a keen and continuing struggle for marketing advantage, they guard the underlying facts and figures about their operations with a secrecy that would do credit to MI5. We were, therefore, unable to collect much useable information from the firms, and have had to rely on two books on detergents and on our own observations and discussions.

The sale of synthetic detergents to industrial users presents few of the features of its marketing to the domestic consumer. The large industrial user is as well-informed about the technical qualities of a detergent as is the seller. He must be persuaded of its superiority over competing brands, and this is often best attempted by personal selling. Advertising has, however, been increasing where it has been found cheaper than personal selling, and it is usually factual and 'informative'.

The very much larger number of domestic buyers makes personal selling impracticable, and advertising is the dominant selling method. Since housewives are not able to compare the technical qualities of competing brands, there may be little point in filling consumer advertising with technical information. The advertising is, therefore, very much of the 'persuasive' kind. But this does not make it contrary to her interests. To say that the housewife is not competent to judge between technical descriptions is not the same as saying that she is not competent to choose between rival brands. All she needs to do is to buy a packet and try it, or rather, buy a packet of each and try them all. The consumer's sovereignty is exercised ex post rather than ex ante. Her choice rests finally with the brand she thinks best – not only for washing her clothes or dishes, but also for ease of use with the washing machine and for the effect on her hands.

Little wonder, then, that the advertising is 'persuasive' in form, with the intention of reminding her constantly of the existence of particular brands and, even more, of developments or improvements in them. Hence the jingles, the rhymes, the slogans – often childish or silly, but presumably judged effective in attracting the housewife's attention.

It is not all silly. A *Financial Times* writer said:[1]

> The intense promotional advertising [of detergents] by Hedley and its competitors during the past few years has been far from indiscriminate, but has been instead the result of careful planning, aimed at a steady overall rise in sales rather than sudden spurts and resulting falls in demand.

Even more effective than a jingle may be the impact of a coupon, a free sample, a free gift, or a localised price-cut. All these serve to get the housewife to try a brand: they are a useful service to her in speeding the rate, and reducing the cost, of acquiring information about the alternatives. It has been found that an inducement to try a new brand is necessary for the conservative British consumer. Perhaps the best apologia for detergent advertising was given by Lord Heyworth in his 1958 address to Unilever shareholders:

> Anything that attempts to change us or jerk us out of our existing habits is apt to be regarded as an irritant. Yet

---

1   *Guaranteed Work in Industry*, 27 January 1955.

although a challenge to go one better than before can be an uncomfortable bed-fellow, it is a prime cause of progress in every field of human life, and it is advertising that brings that challenge home to the individual.

The notion that detergents can be sold simply by assaulting the housewife's mind is wide of the mark. In some areas she rejects brands which do not suit the local water. Some housewives reject brands that are harsh on their hands. Many rejected the early forms of Lever's Wisk and the C.W.S. Cascade because they caked.[2] A survey quoted by Mr Corlett showed that only one in ten housewives shopping at the Co-op bought the C.W.S. detergent.

Detergent advertising is clearly heavy. But detergents cannot be sold at a price low enough to compete with soap unless sales are on a very large scale, and to build up a vast market requires mass advertising. Indeed, to introduce a new brand requires an advertising outlay probably much greater for two or three years than the profits earned on it. Such outlay is a capital investment to be written off over several years and not a cost to be debited against current revenue and included in the price. The market for a new brand is prepared with great care: Hedley usually test-market their brands (i.e. test different selling methods) and introduce them regionally; Unilever normally blind-test their brands (i.e. test housewives' reactions) and introduce them nationally. But neither can be sure how far a new brand will catch on until the whole country or

---

2   Editor's note: C.W.S. was the Co-operative Wholesale Society, now known as the Co-operative Group.

a large part has been informed of it and has tried it: hence advertising and its accompanying introduction methods must be conducted on a large scale.

A further reason for mass advertising is that it is the fastest method of ascertaining how large a market can be built up. Other methods – perhaps house-to-house demonstrations – might be more certain, but they would be too slow.

Advertising may also be cheaper than a price reduction as a market-builder: in most cases its cost would be the same as that incurred from making only a very small price-cut. Furthermore, the effect of a price-cut may soon wear off, and rivals may be able to make similar price reductions but not be able to advertise as heavily or as effectively.

Nevertheless, where the shouting becomes loud and the slogans grow similar, it might seem that the loudest and the 'cleverest' advertiser wins. In 1948, when there were several hundred brands on the market, Unilever, Hedley, Colgate and the C.W.S. accounted for 28 per cent of detergent sales; by 1956 they accounted for 97 per cent, most of it in the hands of Unilever and Hedley. Significantly, during this period total sales increased more than fourfold.

But advertising by itself does not explain why the largest firms have become the dominant suppliers. They had the capital equipment to produce detergents that were technically efficient and of good appearance, did not cake, and had no unpleasant odour. They also had experience of the original soap industry. Not least they could, much better than the powerful chemical and oil-refining companies that supplied the raw materials, ensure efficient distribution through their knowledge of soap marketing and their connections with retail distributors (Unilever, in addition, has an interest in a large number of shops). Indeed marketing – and not merely advertising alone emerges as the key to the understanding of the industry's structure: 'Many people who work in the soap industry consider its principal activity to be the distribution of the soap and synthetic detergent products; they regard the manufacturing side as secondary.'[3]

Objections to detergent advertising are more difficult to resist when they are directed not against the amount of advertising but against its content. Indeed, detergents may provide the example par excellence of products which are so good (and so otherwise expertly marketed) that they can carry the cost of much inferior advertising. The tedious repetition of 'white lies' must surely have long ceased to make the least impact on a large number of viewers and readers. This may be not only wasteful; it has harmful effects on public and political opinion. We have discussed the question of the level at which advertising aims or should aim to be most effective in building sales. This may be a matter of trial and error, but it is difficult to avoid the impression that detergent advertising has been subject to more error than trial: after years of wearisome exaggeration about whiteness and brightness, the public might be excited and parliament impressed if they were shown on television

---

3   W. J. Corlett, op. cit. Both Messrs Puplett and Corlett doubt whether there are appreciable economies of scale in the production of detergents.

the meticulous care in research and product-testing that enable producers to deliver the finest possible detergents. Even if 'hard selling' were not in the long run self-defeating, there are wider political implications to be weighed in the boardroom, where a decision should be taken on how much commercial advantage is worth how much public antipathy and political antagonism.

The market for detergents is an oligopoly (competition between a small number of sellers) or even largely a duopoly (competition between two sellers). But the competition is intense: the two market leaders, Unilever and Hedley (a subsidiary of Procter & Gamble), fight fiercely for markets in most parts of the world, and Hedley boasts that its brands enjoy a large degree of autonomy within the firm and effectively compete with one another. Furthermore, the market leaders are constantly being challenged at some point by Colgate, the C.W.S. and by new firms (several small ones have sold detergents made by Marchon Products). The ultimate safeguard against inflated advertising costs and excessive profits is the power of competitors to offer a better or a noticeably cheaper product.

The aspect which causes concern is the apparent difficulty that small firms capable of offering detergents of equal merit have in entering the market because of the high cost of marketing and research. But, although active competition is limited to three or four firms, potential competition from small firms waiting in the wings, and from large-scale retailers able to integrate backwards, must affect trade policies and limit the capacity to inflate costs and prices. Competition does not have to take place for it to protect the consumer: the threat of competition is the next best thing.

In these circumstances, the weight of advertising will approximate to the amount that offers the best results in building and maintaining market demand. Costs may be inflated, for example, by research designed to evolve differences that will distinguish one brand from others rather than improve its performance, and by heavy advertising of such 'insignificant' differences. But, although the advertising may seem high in total, or as measured in terms of retail value, it is the figure that can be afforded to keep existing brands before the housewife's notice and introduce improvements to keep pace with or ahead of competitors. If the advertising could be reduced without reducing sales so much that earnings were lower, it must be assumed that efforts would be made to reduce it.

In the absence of fuller information, it must be assumed that expenditure on the advertising and marketing of detergents tends towards the optimum in the circumstances prevailing. Sceptics who believe that the advertising could be cut down may not have allowed for its integration with other marketing operations – securing wide distribution (impossible without advertising unless the supplier has a large chain of shops or can win access to them), adjusting retail margins, planning price strategy, arranging displays, samples, coupons, etc., and conducting product tests to keep up with market developments.

The evidence is that the increasing production of detergents by fewer firms has kept prices stable despite the rising costs of raw materials and improved quality in the finished product. Advertising, despite its excesses, has helped (at least in the early stages) to educate the public in the use of a new cleaning agent that has made the chores of the housewife much easier than those of her mother. When detergent advertising is used as a butt by politicians who show no insight into the business problems involved, it is proper to remind ourselves of its economic purpose and of the very great achievements of the British and American entrepreneurs who have, with its help, created a new industry.

APPENDIX B: 'HIDDEN PERSUASION'

Public uneasiness about 'sinister' advertising techniques came to a head with the publication of *Hidden Persuaders* in America and Britain during 1957. The author, Mr Vance Packard, hinted at subtle methods of concealed advertising and political propaganda, and concluded that 'Americans have become the most manipulated people outside the Iron Curtain'. The evidence for this view rested on the most extravagant claims of the extreme psychological school of American practitioners, who have been ridiculed by a British writer, Mr Harry Henry (1958), as 'the wild men of motivation research [...] [who] claim to have the key to the human soul'.

The presentation of the book, with its cover blurb about 'spine-chilling processes evolved and applied by American super-advertising-scientists', led many people, including Professor Aldous Huxley, to confuse the methods of motivation research with the Orwellian possibilities of 'subliminal advertising'.[1] After much alarm had been expressed on the subject, the Institute of Practitioners in Advertising (IPA) set up a committee of enquiry whose report was published in July 1958, under the title *Subliminal Communication*. The committee defined subliminal (or 'sub-threshold')

---

1   In a B.B.C. Brains Trust programme on 26 October, 1958.

communication as 'the deliberate sending of physically weak visual or aural messages of which the recipient is not consciously aware'.

In practice, this means exposing a cinema or television audience to messages repeatedly flashed on the screen for such short periods that they are not noticed by the eye (or if the message is aural it is whispered so quietly that it is not consciously heard). At their simplest, the messages might suggest a certain action – like 'drink', 'smoke' or 'have an ice cream' – and the test is whether the audience shows any measurable response. The IPA committee investigated reports of all experiments published in academic journals, invited the views of prominent psychologists, and arranged for controlled experiments to be conducted by advertising agencies and other commercial research organisations.

According to its report, the committee was unable to discover evidence of any significant measure of success in these experiments. The only claim that subliminal techniques had been used to promote sales came from an interested firm, Subliminal Projection Company, which had been formed to sell such techniques to US advertisers. Its famous 'experiment' in a New Jersey cinema to sell ice cream and popcorn by subliminal suggestion was never substantiated.[2] Yet it was this well-publicised story which, according to *The Spectator*, gave rise to alarm and helped stimulated demand for *Hidden Persuaders*.

2   Editor's footnote: James Vicary, the orchestrator of the popcorn study, later admitted that he had never conducted the subliminal 'experiment' – it was concocted as a gimmick to attract customers to his failing marketing business (O'Barr 2005).

The firm itself has admitted the limitations of subliminal persuasion: it appears that audiences acquire resistance to 'invisible' flashes or 'inaudible' whispers. After reviewing the results of several experiments, the IPA committee concluded that the only one yielding a statistically significant result 'suggested that the audience were avoiding making the choices being suggested by sub-threshold techniques'. In other words, under test conditions, 'hidden persuasion' produced the opposite result to that intended.

Equally significant was the evidence of Professor M. D. Vernon, who stated:

> It is unlikely that even if short-term effects are produced by subthreshold stimulation, there would be any long-term effects unless exactly the same stimulus was repeated frequently in the same form at regular intervals; and unless it led to some form of rewarded behaviour.

Not only does this provide support for the view that consumers know what they want far better than their critics imagine; it also confirms the generally accepted view about hypnosis that subjects of psychological suggestion cannot be induced to behave in ways that are contrary to their own judgement.

Nevertheless, although the IPA committee reported that the dangers of subliminal advertising 'are not justified by any evidence submitted', and that the widely publicised 'case histories' do not exist, it recommended that subliminal methods should not be employed (or experimented with) by its member agencies. The reason given was that 'free choice by the public to accept or reject is an integral part of all forms of professionally acceptable advertising, and [it] does not appear to be available to recipients of subliminal communication'. In July 1958, the IPA Council adopted this report and incorporated a ban on subliminal techniques into the code that binds its members.

In November 1958, questions were asked in the House of Commons about the alleged use of subliminal advertising by the Welsh television programme contractor. After repeating the denial by the company that such methods had been used, the Postmaster General made it clear that they would be contrary to the provisions of the Television Act.

Undoubtedly, the ban is a proper safeguard against possible 'underhand' methods of influencing the public, which could be even more dangerous if used for political rather than commercial ends. We have argued that the public is more robust-minded than over-sensitive critics allow, but it can be on guard against commercial persuasion only so long as the source of the advertisement can be detected.

Although the most authoritative investigation so far conducted on subliminal persuasion provided evidence not of the wickedness of advertisers but of the readiness of critics to think the worst of them, the advertising business must not be too cavalier in dismissing these criticisms. Though the IPA moved to meet the exaggerated fears about 'hidden persuasion' quickly, it might have done better to have invited independent experts to serve on the committee of enquiry, instead of confining its membership to advertising people. There remains the need to reassure the public that a continuing watch will be maintained to prevent any possibility of unscrupulous advertisers or media owners seeking to employ subliminal techniques.

APPENDIX C: POLITICAL ADVERTISING

In a Commons debate on protection for the consumer, Mr Anthony Greenwood, leading for the Opposition, chose to compare advertising with political propaganda. After ridiculing the claims made by detergent manufacturers, he concluded: 'I have no doubt that there are many people who are deceived by this detergent advertising, just as at election times, unfortunately they are deceived by propaganda from the [Conservative] Party opposite.' Implicit in this statement is the view that, whilst his political opponents make misleading or false claims about their intentions and record, Mr Greenwood's Party laboured under the disadvantage of telling the truth about their policies. Before examining some of the evidence for this claim, we shall enquire whether advertising and propaganda may be compared in this way.

Lindley Fraser, who acquired massive experience of the subject as chief commentator of the BBC German service during the war, has defined propaganda as aimed at 'inducing desired behaviour in others', and devoted a chapter of his book to advertising, under the heading 'Commercial Propaganda'. He contrasted 'salesmanship' with advertising, the former being a personal approach to individuals and relying more on reasoned argument, the latter being a mass appeal and generally directed to collective emotions rather than to intellect. In this sense advertising has much in common with the techniques of propaganda, although those who think this makes advertising more vulnerable to criticism should read Mr Fraser's analysis of the limitations of advertising. He argued persuasively that, in anything but the very short run, lies are poor propaganda unless the victims have no means of checking or verification (as in totalitarian countries), or unless the propagandist is appealing to a really urgent hope and will be heard uncritically (as with an invalid who buys a drug pedlar's panacea). In general Mr Fraser concluded that legal and voluntary measures have brought an approximation to truthfulness in advertising. Historically, he claimed, advertising has made the Western democracies 'progress-minded': he contrasted the old-fashioned resistance to new-fangled devices (such as typewriters and telephones) with the modern readiness 'to accept and even welcome yet further changes in material ways of living'.

If, then, there is a close analogy between advertising and political propaganda, we can examine Mr Greenwood's implied claim that the Labour Party practices truthfulness in its appeal to the electorate. The following are examples of statements made by Labour spokesmen (sometimes Labour headquarters itself) when seeking to 'sell' socialism at the price of no more than a vote.

Appeals to hope

1944: Before Mr Herbert Morrison had formally buried 'the old scarcity economics', an official Labour pamphlet *Your*

Future After Victory (in the form of a conversation piece) told a war-weary, austerity-ridden public: 'Now, I will say straight away that you can have all you want. The Labour Party says there is no reason why everyone in the land [...] should not have everything which goes to make a full, happy and secure life.'

1945: Messrs Bevin, Cripps, Dalton, Shinwell, Strauss, and others joined in promising that nationalisation would bring cheaper coal, electricity and transport. On housing they differed only on whether a Labour Government would build four, five or six million houses in a few years (when after six years fewer than one million new houses had been built it became fashionable to talk of 'accommodation units').

Appeals to fear

The 'dole queue' has served Labour propagandists as the fear card to play on every favourable occasion: predictions have varied from 'mass unemployment' to 'a million or more' (forecast in 1956 by the moderate Mr Robens).

Since 1950 fear of war and annihilation has taken first place in the Labour Party's election appeals. 'Reach for a rifle, or reach old age' was the choice posed in 1951. One Labour candidate thought a more graphic presentation would be to show a cemetery with the caption: 'Your X can save a million crosses'. If anything, less subtle, was the warning against Mr Churchill, 'a man of blood' who 'has lived on war like a vulture lives on dead', uttered by a Labour candidate who was judged a fitting opponent to R. A.

Butler in 1950. Mr Sidney Silverman showed himself an imaginative political copy-writer when, in 1951, he warned the country that if Labour lost, Britain would go 'back with the Tories to the blood bath, the shambles and the abyss'.

The official posters have specialised in portraying bonny babies who testify that they owe their health, even their existence, to the Labour Party. The broadsheet which reproduced a picture of the infant Duke of Kent, taken in 1936, as an example of a bonny Socialist baby in 1949 was an honest if clumsy error for which indulgence was sought, but which would have doomed a private advertiser for all time.

Health claims abound in the gallery of Labour posters. Nursing mothers have appealed to be saved from the Tories – 'For safer motherhood, vote Labour' – and babies themselves have been exploited to beg voters to 'take care of us'. Are the ethics of advertising worse than this? A variation of the health theme was to portray doctors and nurses who lent their anonymous authority to debatable assertions and statistics.

The 1956 version of truth in Labour propaganda

During 1956 the Labour Party published two leaflets: one to shed light on the living standards under Conservative misrule, the other to sum up the great debate of the Rent Act. The first showed a mother talking to a child in a high chair and saying: 'No, you can't have bread and milk – d'you think we're made of money?' The other described the Rent Act as 'a present which will total nearly £100 million is to be contributed by nearly every tenant in Britain to landlords [...]'.

No doubt equally misleading quotations could be selected from statements made by spokesmen for the Conservative Party (and in its heyday by Liberal Party propagandists). Such an exercise would merely serve to illustrate that, at their worst, politicians are no more scrupulous and often less scrupulous than advertisers bidding for mass support, in exaggerating the favourable aspects of their wares and concealing the unfavourable. It has become a fusty fallacy to suppose that moral standards are higher in political than in commercial life.

Politicians who preach honesty to business men display no great enthusiasm to tell the 'whole truth'. In presenting their case they give prominence to some facets and blandly suppress others. The important difference in method between political and commercial advertising is that the politician specialises in disparaging his rival whereas the ban against 'knocking copy' drives the advertiser to concentrate on the positive attractions of his product, leaving the customer to draw his own conclusions about the implied criticism of others.

In principle there is much similarity in the techniques employed. The pressure of competition between rival products invites claims no less extreme or exaggerated than those thrown up in the battle between rival policies. Viewed in this light, it may appear remarkable not that advertisers 'speak well of themselves' but that, largely through self-imposed restraint, they avoid some of the grosser insults to our intelligence that politicians daily feel driven to perpetrate. Is it more important that the public should select the right detergent than that it should make an informed choice between rival economic and social policies at election time? Yet that seems to be the view of politicians who wish to impose a far higher standard on advertisers than they accept for themselves. Perhaps, after all, people may be credited with more discernment than Mr Greenwood allows.

The comparative ethics of commercial and political life is a dangerous subject for the politician to embark upon, especially for the politician who wants more and more power over the economic destinies of his fellow citizens. Indeed, it is precisely because the 'politicalisation' of economic life would intensify its defects, or replace them by worse ones, that the free economy is superior to the state-directed economy.

APPENDIX D: A SUBSIDISED PRESS?

Fears for the survival of a vigorous free press are increased if the advocates of an advertising tax are assumed to be more concerned to reduce advertising than to raise revenue. When the Fabian Professor Arthur Lewis in *The Economics of Overhead Costs* visualised deliberate measures to reduce advertising expenditure, he acknowledged that the press would shrivel unless the government stepped in with subsidies, distributed perhaps on the basis of circulation.

Some might be tempted to view such a development with complacency on the grounds that the press would merely be receiving a subsidy from a different source. But there is a world of difference between receiving money from a large number of competing private businesses and receiving all of it from one political source. Talk about the pressure of advertisers on editorial opinion misses this point. There may be examples of improper pressure, and a particular item of news may be emphasised or suppressed out of deference to advertisers. But this is as nothing compared with the prostitution of the press for political purposes that would accompany government subsidies. Nor does the fact that newspapers now receive between 50 per cent and 60 per cent of their income from advertising justify the use of the word 'subsidy'. A subsidy is a payment made by a third party which artificially reduces the price of a commodity to customers. But the payment made by advertisers for press space is a straightforward commercial payment. It is not an act of benevolence but of business: the advertiser pays for value received or anticipated. It is true that the reader pays less for his paper than he would in the absence of advertising, but so does a train passenger pay a lower fare than he would if there were fewer travellers and less freight to contribute towards the overhead costs of the service. Economic life is full of similar examples.

As Francis Williams makes clear in his *Dangerous Estate*, advertisements are an integral part of a newspaper. 'They are news,' wrote F. P. Bishop, 'varying of course like other contents of a paper in interest and importance.' Indeed much financial and legal advertising is required by statute as the most effective way of publicising notices (about bankruptcies, wills, share issues, official appointments, etc.). If there were no suitable newspapers, and trustees had to canvass round for creditors, etc., the cost would be far greater than inserting a public notice in the appropriate columns.

It is no coincidence that the spread of a free press dates from the rise of commercial advertising a hundred years ago. Whatever consequences an advertising tax would have for modern industry and commerce, its effects upon the British press could not be other than damaging and might prove disastrous.

APPENDIX E: RESTRICTIVE PRACTICES IN PRINTING AND THEIR EFFECTS ON ADVERTISING COSTS[1]

Lack of advertising is only one reason for the demise of many newspapers and periodicals in recent years. More important are the conditions within the printing industry itself; in particular the high cost of newsprint, paper and overheads, especially for labour.

The big newspapers are able to absorb these costs without raising prices unduly because their circulations automatically attract large advertising revenue. Hence their managements permit restrictive practices for the sake of industrial peace in an industry in which every day is vital. This makes the problem of costs all the more difficult for provincial papers and periodicals which lack the large circulations necessary to secure comfortable advertising revenues, but which have to pay the extravagant costs tolerated by the proprietors of leading national papers.

Employees themselves must bear a share of the responsibility for the trend towards monopoly of ownership in the newspaper industry. Costs are unnecessarily raised by trade agreements and restrictive practices in many newspaper offices. For example, after leaving the editorial floor,

---

1   This note is based upon a memorandum prepared by a journalist employed in a large newspaper office.

the copy prepared by journalists and the advertising department goes to the composing room for setting. There are three types of operatives who set copy: Linotype operators, 'stab' hands, and case men. All belong to a craft union which is one of the several that restrict entry into the printing industry with the connivance of the employer. The Linotype operators are piece-workers paid on the amount of type they set and pool their earnings. The case men, who set headlines and advertisements, are also piece-workers.

Many advertisements are sent to printing offices from the advertising agencies as 'stereos', which are metal plates containing all the type, pictures, drawings, etc., that are to go into the advertisements. There is no need for the case room to set any of this type, but the case room men charge for the entire setting. And if the same advertisement runs in the newspaper for more than one day, the case room men may charge for each day on which it is published.

The 'stab' hands are responsible for making up the pages and placing the type as directed in the lay-outs designed by editorial executives. If a block of a picture needs trimming in size they are not allowed to move it out of the metal page. The stereo men insist on trimming the mounting of the block, even when this delay would make the paper late.

By and large, men in the composing room are not responsible for excessive piling up of costs, though many old practices die hard in an industry which has had an extremely strong trade union organisation since the 18th century. Restrictive practices are more common in the sections responsible for printing and dispatch.

Automation has, of course, reached the machine rooms of Britain's printing offices, but managements experience great difficulties with unions in cutting down the number of staff employed. The Royal Commission on the Press was told of an American who visited a machine room in a British newspaper office, and found a machine exactly like one used in America. But, though five Americans worked the machine, the number employed in Britain was thirteen or fourteen.

Process workers (the men who make blocks of photographs and cartoons, etc.) have agreements which differ from office to office. In some cases if their work requires ten minutes overtime they have to be paid for three hours. Restrictive practices abound in the stereo department which makes the metal plates of the made-up pages for use on the rotary printing machines. Some men are engaged solely in putting plates of pages on lifts. If these go to the foundry late, the whole section charges over-time though some of the men will have no work to do.

Over-employment is greatest in the use of unskilled and semi-skilled labour. Many of these employees belong to the National Society of Operative Printers and Assistants (NATSOPA), and are found in almost every department of the large newspaper. The skilled men in the editorial department comprise executives, feature writers, sub-editors, reporters and photographers. Almost without exception, they are members of the National Union of Journalists or the Institute of Journalists, the professional bodies which exist for writers and photographers. But, this department includes telephone copy typists, secretaries, teleprinter assistants and copy runners and messengers – classified as editorial assistants. They are members of NATSOPA.

Many employees in the readers' department belong to NATSOPA, whose members are also found in the composing room where they act as messengers and as pullers of rough proofs.

Another union has members in the machine room – pushing papers along for dispatch, one man to every yard. Much of the labour employed here is on a casual basis, and agreements are made under which a specified number of men are used every day whether or not they are required. There is a classic story of a barman who works in a public house close to some of the large newspaper offices in Fleet Street being called from behind the bar to 'sign on', and then going straight back to pull his pints.

Many of these workers are required only in short stretches (when the papers are printed and come off the machines), but they have to be paid for a full shift. It has been known for men employed at one Sunday newspaper office to sign on before going to a dog race meeting and return in time to carry out their 'work'.

To cover inflated costs at every stage in the printing of papers the advertiser obviously has to pay heavily. Prosperous proprietors tolerate these restrictions in the knowledge that the agencies will pay; the agencies pay, deduct larger commissions and pass the bill to the advertiser. It is time that advertisers, as the chief paymasters of all employed in printing, exerted their influence to secure better value for their money.

APPENDIX F: THE BATTLE FOR COMMERCIAL TELEVISION – WHO WAS RIGHT?

Forecasts

1952: Labour Party leaflet 'Not Fit for Children' incited readers: 'Protest to your MP. Warn your neighbours and friends against the Conservative TV (too vulgar) policy'.

1953: Christopher Mayhew in a pamphlet entitled 'Dear Viewer' warned 'Commercialism ruins T.V. standards [...] such a step would be a real disaster for this country'.

1954: Lord Hailsham urged the House of Lords to 'reject this evil, mischievous, ill-considered Bill [...]' which Lord Simon of Wythenshawe denounced as opening up 'a terrifying prospect'. Sir Robert Fraser, the Director General of the Independent Television Authority (ITA), forecast: 'Free television should now evolve on principles that will place it beside our free press, our free books and our free arts, as a normal part of the equipment of our free society'.

Results

1958: Sir Robert Fraser reported that the ITA contractors were first to provide 'regular nation-wide television schools programmes in the English-speaking world'. After two-and-a-half years of competition for his attention, the British viewer could choose from '120 hours of programmes each week instead of only 35, which was the output of British television in its twelfth year [...] In any typical period of ten weeks in 1955 [before there were two services] the viewer looking for programmes of religion would have found four, one church service and three discussion programmes. In a similar ten week period now, he would find thirty-two, twelve church or chapel services and twenty discussion programmes'.

In a detailed comparison of the BBC output before September, 1955, with that of both BBC and ITA in 1958, Sir Robert Fraser showed that the weekly number of serious programmes had developed as follows: 10–15 in the BBC service before ITA; 18–22 in the present BBC service; 18–20 in the present ITA service. The total in both services is therefore about 36–42, which is three times the output of serious programmes in the days of the BBC television monopoly.

On the broader issues, Sir Robert Fraser concluded: 'By no argument of which I can conceive is it possible to reconcile monopoly in broadcasting [...] with the faith of a free man in freedom. I believe that, in the fundamental sense, the great advances in British television secured since 1954, not least it would seem to me, in the BBC service itself, are the fruits of freedom. And I rejoice that few, if any, in Britain would now ever dream of reimposing the rule of monopoly which came to an end only thirty short months ago'.

REFERENCES

Abbott, L. (1956) *Quality and Competition*. Columbia University Press.

Adler, M. (1956) *Modern Market Research*. London: Crosby Lockwood & Son.

Andrews, P. W. S. (1949) *Manufacturing Business*. London: Macmillan.

Baster, A. S. J. (1935) *Advertising Reconsidered*. London: King & Son.

Baster, A. S. J. (1947) *The Little Less*. London: Methuen.

Baynes, M. (1956) *Advertising on Trial*. London: Bow Group.

Bell, D. 1956 *The Listener*, 27 December.

Bishop, F. P. (1944) *Economics of Advertising*. London: Robert Hale.

Bishop, F. P. (1949) *Ethics of Advertising*. London: Robert Hale.

Bishop, F. P. (1952) *Advertising and the Law*. London: Benn.

Borden, N. H. (1952) *Economic Effects of Advertising*. R. D. Irwin (1942).

Brandon, R. (1955) *Costing for Advertising*. London: Bailey & Swinfen.

Chamberlain, E. H. (1935) *The Theory of Monopolistic Competition*. Cambridge, MA: Harvard University Press.

Fortune (ed.) (1957) *The Amazing Advertising Business*. New York: Simon & Schuster.

Fraser, Sir Robert (1958) *Two Years of Independent Television, and Other Collected Speeches*. ITA.

Galbraith, J. K. (1958) *The Affluent Society*. London: Hamish Hamilton.

Hall, M. (1949) *Distributive Trading*. London: Hutchinson.

Harbury, C. D. (1958) *Efficiency and the Consumer*. London: Fabian Society.

Henry, H. (1958) *Motivation Research*. London: Crosby Lockwood & Son.

Hobson, J. W. (1955) *Selection of Advertising Media*. Business Publications.

Jefferys, J. B. (1954) *Retail Trading in Britain 1850–1950*. Cambridge University Press.

Jewkes, J. (1948) *Ordeal by Planning*. London: Macmillan.

Jewkes, J., Sawers, D. and Stillerman, R. (1958) *The Sources of Invention*. London: Macmillan.

Kaldor, N. and Silverman, S. (1948) *Statistical Analysis of Advertising Expenditure*. Cambridge University Press.

Kaldor, N. (1950) The economics of advertising. *Review of Economic Studies* 18: 1–27.

Knight, F. (1921) *Risk, Uncertainty and Profit*. New York: Harper and Row.

Knight, F. (1935) *Ethics of Competition*. London: Allen & Unwin.

Laski, M. (1958) *The Twentieth Century*, April.

Lever, E. A. (1947) *Advertising and Economic Theory*. Oxford University Press.

Lewis, W. A. (1945) Competition in retail trade. *Economica* 12 (48).

Lewis, W. A. (1949) *Overhead Costs*. London: Allen & Unwin.

Milne, A. (1956) Organising advertising in Britain, *Journal of the Advertising Association*, 30th anniversary issue, February.

Northcott, J. F. (1953) *Value for Money?* London: Fabian Society.

O'Barr, W. (2005) 'Subliminal' advertising. *Advertising and Society Review* 6(4).

Plant, A. (1937) The distribution of proprietary articles. In *Some Modern Business Problems*. London: Longmans Green.

Pigou, A. (1920) *The Economics of Welfare*. London: Macmillan.

Robbins, L. (1952) *The Theory of Economic Policy*. London: Macmillan.

Robertson, Sir Dennis (1958) *Lectures on Economic Principles*. London: Staples Press.

Robinson, J. (1933) *Economics of Imperfect Competition*. London: Macmillan.

Waite, W. C. and Cassady, R. (1949) *The Consumer and the Economic Order*. New York: McGraw-Hill.

Waterhouse, K. (1958) *Future of Television*. Spotlight pamphlet published by the *Daily Mirror*.

Williams, F. (1957) *Dangerous Estate*. London: Longmans.

Yamey, B. S. (1954a) *Economics of Resale Price Maintenance*. London: Pitman.

Yamey, B. S. (1954b) The evolution of shopkeeping. *Lloyds Bank Review*, January.

ABOUT THE IEA

The Institute is a research and educational charity (No. CC 235 351), limited by guarantee. Its mission is to improve understanding of the fundamental institutions of a free society by analysing and expounding the role of markets in solving economic and social problems.

The IEA achieves its mission by:

- a high-quality publishing programme
- conferences, seminars, lectures and other events
- outreach to school and college students
- brokering media introductions and appearances

The IEA, which was established in 1955 by the late Sir Antony Fisher, is an educational charity, not a political organisation. It is independent of any political party or group and does not carry on activities intended to affect support for any political party or candidate in any election or referendum, or at any other time. It is financed by sales of publications, conference fees and voluntary donations.

In addition to its main series of publications the IEA also publishes a quarterly journal, *Economic Affairs*.

The IEA is aided in its work by a distinguished international Academic Advisory Council and an eminent panel of Honorary Fellows. Together with other academics, they review prospective IEA publications, their comments being passed on anonymously to authors. All IEA papers are therefore subject to the same rigorous independent refereeing process as used by leading academic journals.

IEA publications enjoy widespread classroom use and course adoptions in schools and universities. They are also sold throughout the world and often translated/reprinted.

Since 1974 the IEA has helped to create a worldwide network of 100 similar institutions in over 70 countries. They are all independent but share the IEA's mission.

Views expressed in the IEA's publications are those of the authors, not those of the Institute (which has no corporate view), its Managing Trustees, Academic Advisory Council members or senior staff.

Members of the Institute's Academic Advisory Council, Honorary Fellows, Trustees and Staff are listed on the following page.

The Institute gratefully acknowledges financial support for its publications programme and other work from a generous benefaction by the late Professor Ronald Coase.

Other papers recently published by the IEA include:

Does Britain Need a Financial Regulator?
Statutory Regulation, Private Regulation and Financial Markets
Terry Arthur & Philip Booth
Hobart Paper 169; ISBN 978-0-255-36593-2; £12.50

Hayek's The Constitution of Liberty
An Account of Its Argument
Eugene F. Miller
Occasional Paper 144; ISBN 978-0-255-36637-3; £12.50

Fair Trade Without the Froth
A Dispassionate Economic Analysis of 'Fair Trade'
Sushil Mohan
Hobart Paper 170; ISBN 978-0-255-36645-8; £10.00

A New Understanding of Poverty
Poverty Measurement and Policy Implications
Kristian Niemietz
Research Monograph 65; ISBN 978-0-255-36638-0; £12.50

The Challenge of Immigration
A Radical Solution
Gary S. Becker
Occasional Paper 145; ISBN 978-0-255-36613-7; £7.50

Sharper Axes, Lower Taxes
Big Steps to a Smaller State
Edited by Philip Booth
Hobart Paperback 38; ISBN 978-0-255-36648-9; £12.50

Self-employment, Small Firms and Enterprise
Peter Urwin
Research Monograph 66; ISBN 978-0-255-36610-6; £12.50

Crises of Governments
The Ongoing Global Financial Crisis and Recession
Robert Barro
Occasional Paper 146; ISBN 978-0-255-36657-1; £7.50

... and the Pursuit of Happiness
Wellbeing and the Role of Government
Edited by Philip Booth
Readings 64; ISBN 978-0-255-36656-4; £12.50

Public Choice – A Primer
Eamonn Butler
Occasional Paper 147; ISBN 978-0-255-36650-2; £10.00

The Profit Motive in Education: Continuing the Revolution
Edited by James B. Stanfield
Readings 65; ISBN 978-0-255-36646-5; £12.50

Which Road Ahead – Government or Market?
Oliver Knipping & Richard Wellings
Hobart Paper 171; ISBN 978-0-255-36619-9; £10.00

The Future of the Commons
Beyond Market Failure and Government Regulation
Elinor Ostrom et al.
Occasional Paper 148; ISBN 978-0-255-36653-3; £10.00

Redefining the Poverty Debate
Why a War on Markets Is No Substitute for a War on Poverty
Kristian Niemietz
Research Monograph 67; ISBN 978-0-255-36652-6; £12.50

The Euro – the Beginning, the Middle ... and the End?
Edited by Philip Booth
Hobart Paperback 39; ISBN 978-0-255-36680-9; £12.50

The Shadow Economy
Friedrich Schneider & Colin C. Williams
Hobart Paper 172; ISBN 978-0-255-36674-8; £12.50

Quack Policy
Abusing Science in the Cause of Paternalism
Jamie Whyte
Hobart Paper 173; ISBN 978-0-255-36673-1; £10.00

Foundations of a Free Society
Eamonn Butler
Occasional Paper 149; ISBN 978-0-255-36687-8; £12.50

The Government Debt Iceberg
Jagadeesh Gokhale
Research Monograph 68; ISBN 978-0-255-36666-3; £10.00

A U-Turn on the Road to Serfdom
Grover Norquist
Occasional Paper 150; ISBN 978-0-255-36686-1; £10.00

New Private Monies – A Bit-Part Player?
Kevin Dowd
Hobart Paper 174; ISBN 978-0-255-36694-6; £10.00

From Crisis to Confidence – Macroeconomics after the Crash
Roger Koppl
Hobart Paper 175; ISBN 978-0-255-36693-9; £12.50

Other IEA publications

Comprehensive information on other publications and the wider work of the IEA can be found at www.iea.org.uk. To order any publication please see below.

Personal customers

Orders from personal customers should be directed to the IEA:

Clare Rusbridge
IEA
2 Lord North Street
FREEPOST LON10168
London SW1P 3YZ
Tel: 020 7799 8907. Fax: 020 7799 2137
Email: sales@iea.org.uk

Trade customers

All orders from the book trade should be directed to the IEA's distributor:

NBN International (IEA Orders)
Orders Dept.
NBN International
10 Thornbury Road
Plymouth PL6 7PP
Tel: 01752 202301, Fax: 01752 202333
Email: orders@nbninternational.com

IEA subscriptions

The IEA also offers a subscription service to its publications. For a single annual payment (currently £42.00 in the UK), subscribers receive every monograph the IEA publishes. For more information please contact:

Clare Rusbridge
Subscriptions
IEA
2 Lord North Street
FREEPOST LON10168
London SW1P 3YZ
Tel: 020 7799 8907, Fax: 020 7799 2137
Email: crusbridge@iea.org.uk